A
GOOD MEDICINE
COLLECTION

Life in Harmony with Nature

Adolf Hungry Wolf

Previously Published as
Parts of the Good Medicine
Books Series, Volumes 1, 2, 4, 6 & 8

Good Medicine Books
Skookumchuck, B.C., Canada

1983

Hungry Wolf, Adolf

A Good Medicine Collection
1. Indians of North America
2. Natural lifestyles
3. Philosophy

ISBN 0-920698-36-0

FOREWORD

Many Summers and Winters have passed since I first wrote down the stories and thoughts in this book. We have all made changes in that time, and we are wondering what is coming our way in the seasons ahead. It seems that life may be altered drastically, soon. And yet, we are surrounded by a vast timelessness that makes our present and future seem so insignificant. . . .

But no matter how the world develops, people continue to be fascinated by nature. The theme of this book is living in harmony with nature. Its contents are meant to inspire you to think about our relationships with the Earth, the Universe, and each other. Many of us dream of a time when all people again learn to live in harmony with nature, even though the actual possibility of this seems to get more remote with the passing of every year. Some say this is too romantic, but would they suggest that we should not dream?

These writings are intended to be a tribute to native American people. Harmony with nature has always been the goal of their traditional life. Today it is also the goal of many others, who would prefer to see the continent return to such a life rather than be further destroyed.

The spirit of life in harmony with nature is within each of us, whether our ancestors were native Americans, native Europeans, native Asians, or native Africans. In primitive times they all practiced tribal lifestyles in nature. When I came to America as a boy, in the 1950's, I felt like a cultural orphan. My European ancestors had given up their traditional life in nature so long ago that there was virtually nothing left for me to learn about it. Like many others, I looked with admiration at native American culture, which seemed so close to its natural past.

Throughout my school years I daydreamed about tribal and cultural life, wondering if it was possible to reverse the social trend back towards nature. I studied books and read magazines on the subject, and later learned directly from native elders, themselves. They said dreams are challenges in life that should be fulfilled. I married one of their granddaughters, and together we try teaching our children to fulfill their dreams with love for nature and the earth.

With my family I have written many more things since the thoughts and stories in this book. I thought these early writings might become forgotten, but readers continue to request them, so now they are reprinted into this single volume. But then, I also thought cultural lifestyles would fade into the past. . . . Their recent revival makes me glad to admit that I was wrong!

A.H.W.
Spring, 1983

If You are Seeking the True meanings of the many aspects of Life then Go into Nature. Go where You can enjoy evenings studying the Stars from the porch of your own home, on your own land. Go where You can see the trees that provide the lumber for your house. Go where You can see the crops that provide the food for your table. Go where You can follow the stream that provides your water. Go where You can wander for hours and think freely. Go where You can enjoy directly the fruits of your labor. Go and become what YOU think You are.

Are You clinging to the breast of ready-made living? Are You *afraid* to lose the "comforts" of such living by removing yourself to an unadulterated environment in Nature? Be honest with yourself--have you *really* even thought about changing your way of life? Not just daydreamed and speculated, but really *thought* about it? It isn't hard to change and it's *never* too late. *All* You have to do is set Your Mind on it! Review the factors in your present life. Review the factors of alternate lives. Let the facts make your decision, then let your Mind be your guide. Remember:

You Are What YOU Think You Are

Do you really think that You can be satisfied with your life if you spend the most important hours of the next *Forty Years* away from your family, your home, and your personal Self? Do You really believe that the benefits gained from selling your time to others are worth more to you than that time itself? Do you have to earn money so that you can pay others to do for you those things which you haven't the time to do yourself because you are busy earning money?

Decide Now that You want to have more time to Experience the many Natural aspects of True Life. Set your Mind to it. Save your money and buy a piece of land somewhere where the only thing between Earth and the Universe is You. Grow some crops. Raise some chickens and goats. Go to town occasionally for your supplies. Stop wondering about the ingredients of a bowl of soup - - produce the ingredients yourself. Stop worrying about the taste of water - - obtain that water yourself. Stop wondering what's inside the walls of your house- - put those walls up yourself.

You owe it to your Life and the Life of your Family to consider the alternatives to acting as a cog in the world of mechanization. Don't let the intricacies of mechanical wonders amaze you into accepting them blindly as substitutes for processes of Life over which You should have direct knowledge and control.

WHAT IS GOOD MEDICINE

To understand the real meaning of the term GOOD MEDICINE, One must first realize the importance of the spiritualism that can be found in everything Natural. It is thus that People living in Nature can make a religion of their daily lives. GOOD MEDICINE means a Positive Spiritual Life. GOOD MEDICINE means realizing that there is more to Life than meets the eye. Belief in GOOD MEDICINE is one answer to the need that People in Nature find for expressing their humbleness to all that surrounds them.

Many people have asked, and others thought they answered: What do People believe when they live with Medicine--what do they pray to? They should learn that Medicine is not a subject for scholarly dissection, for it has no universal answers. For instance, tribal beliefs in North America varied widely. They depended mainly on the environment and daily pursuits of the People. Imagine the basic differences between the Arapahoe, who hunted Buffalo on the open plains, the Hopi, who still raise corn in the hot deserts, and the Seminole, who hunt and harvest in swamps and jungles. In addition to these tribal differences, caused by physical factors, were the personal differences, caused by mental factors. For the ultimate interpretation of spiritual life must be left to the worshipping individual. It must depend on his spiritual awareness.

As all Truths must come from within the Mind, it is good to spend many times alone with the Mind. This is readily done in the Sanctuary of Nature. Thus, the follower of Medicine goes into the Great Outdoors with the same awe and respect that another would have upon entering an ancient cathedral.

The profound spiritual experience sought by those who follow the traditional belief in the Great Power of Nature is the Vision Experience. Visions, in this case, are those things experienced by the Mind when one is dreaming--when one allows the Mind to wander freely, without thoughts of social or physical restrictions. At such times many subconscious thoughts and abilities express themselves in the Mind.

The most sought-for Visions have been of visits with some spiritual element of Nature: a bird, an animal, a stone, or a star. Some have considered Visions of certain elements more powerful than others, but such decisions should only be made in the individual's own Mind. The Vision visit usually includes the ceremonial smoking of a pipe, the singing of songs, the performance of a ritual, and instructions to make or find certain objects and when to carry them. The ceremonies and material objects may later serve as physical reminders of one's spiritual ally, to provide comfort in a vast Universe where one may, at times, feel quite alone.

YOUNG STABS-BY-MISTAKE ~ PIKUNI

It has often been said that Medicine is a pagan belief that involves the use of witchcraft spells and weird physical doctoring. These claims have generally been made by un-Aware observers, who understood spiritual activity only as it was described in the rule-books of their own religions. One cannot write objectively about the spiritual beliefs of another's religion when he thinks that only *his* religion is "the right one."

First, witchcraft should not be confused with emotional spiritual experiences, which the followers of Medicine often seek. Further-more, any power to perform physical doctoring had to come through very strong Dreams, and was often limited to the treatment of specific ailments. Relatively few Medicine Men were given such Power, and these were usually wise ones well versed in plant lore and human physiology. People living in a healthy, Natural environ-ment have more need for spiritual guidance than medical help.

Visions might come at any time, during any kind of experience. Most properly, however, Visions are Sought during a Vision Quest. With preparation, one goes to a favorite and secluded place in Nature to meditate. Often a Vision Seeker goes forth with a specific element in Mind with which he would like to visit in Dream- -the one he would most like to have as his spiritual ally. A powerful Vision experience requires intimate aquaintance with the physical aspects of the Seeker's environment. He should know the names and uses of plants and berries, the sounds and habits of birds and animals, and the signs of weather and terrain. This way, he will be familiar with the elements encountered in the Vision, and know which aspects are to be most respected.

Most everyone who has spent any time out in Nature knows the feeling of an Unseen Presence. Such a feeling leads one to question what signs of the past may be visible and what unseen presence may still be there. It is good to question these things. It is good to realize that this kind of spiritual feeling is proof of a Power be-yond that which is physical.

When you find a particularly moving spiritual place in Nature- - one where you easily sense more than physical powers- -then spend some time there. Stand before a large tree there, or sit on a big boulder. Realize YOUR place in the existance of all this. You should be humbled. Seek what others before you may have sought there also- -look around for what might give spiritual guid-ance and motivation. Look Up at the Sky. Look Down at the Earth. Study the movements of Clouds. Study the details of Pebbles. See how beautiful this simple, Natural Life around you is. Ask yourself how You might permanently become a part of this beautiful Life.

Ask aloud how You might find a place in Nature. Ask aloud many times, and observe All that surrounds you. Become Aware of the Powers that you can see, and allow the unseen Powers to make You aware of their presence, too. Do this for an hour. Do this for a full day. When you have come to know Your place by daylight, stay there for a night. Do not fear Nature because you cannot see its details in the dark. Fear is only in your Mind. Give your Mind to Nature, as you become aquainted with Nature--*do not* try to control it with facts and figures learned in another environment. Do not discredit spiritual thoughts in your Mind with physical reasoning. Do not become distracted by thoughts of eating or sleeping--do them Naturally, if such becomes your desire. Spend your time singing, chanting, talking, and listening--all the while watching and thinking. Let the forces of Nature Guide your Awareness----*Respect That Guidance!*

If your eyes tend to distract your Mind from entering the spiritual realm, find some intriguing object to concentrate your Vision upon. Let that object filter the thoughts which enter and leave your Mind. Find a small stone, a seed, a piece of wood, or a bird's feather. Decorate it by polishing with your fingers or by attaching beads. Allow a ritual- short or long- to develop Naturally, whereby your Mind is cleared of all but spiritual thoughts. Use this as your key to the door of the spiritual world. YOU *can* do it, if Your desires are strong enough!

> *RELEASE YOUR MIND TO NATURE:*
> *Let Us Meet There. . . .*
> *Let Us Meet The Others There. . . .*
> *Let US ALL Be There Together. . .*

BRAVE BUFFALO'S DREAM

One's Medicine is a very sacred thing--not to be discussed lightly, or with just any person. Some people never reveal to anyone the details of their personal spiritual power. Here is the story of a Medicine Dream that was told by an old Sioux Medicine Man named Brave Buffalo (Tatan' ka ohi' tika) shortly before his death:

When I was 10 years of age I looked at the land and the rivers, the sky above, and the animals around me and could not fail to realize that they were made by some great power. I was so anxious to understand this power that I questioned the trees and the bushes. It seemed as though the flowers were staring at me, and I wanted to ask them "Who made you?" I looked at the moss-covered stones; some of them seemed to have the features of a man, but they could not answer me. Then I had a Dream, and in my Dream one of these small round stones appeared to me and told me that the maker of All was Wakan' Tanka (Great Spirit of the Sioux), and that in order to honor Him I must honor His works in Nature. The stone then said that by my search I had shown myself worthy of supernatural help, and that it would provide for me this help.

Brave Buffalo found a physical specimen similar to his Dream rock, which he covered with an Eagle down feather and wrapped in a piece of buckskin. Its presence reminded him of the strength promised in the Dream. Such objects may be attached to a buckskin thong and worn around the neck. Several Medicine objects may be included within one wrapping. When too many objects accumulate, or the size of an object becomes too large, a fringed buckskin bag or a cylindrical rawhide case may be used as a container. Wrapped with pieces of gaily color-ed cloth, silk neckerchiefs, or finely-tanned furs, the objects may become part of a Medicine Bun-dle. Such Bundles are never unwrapped with-out purpose, pipe smoking, incense burning, songs, and prayers. They are generally hung, along with other Medicine objects, on a wooden tripod by the owner's bed. Incense is burned by them daily.

To the right is a Crow man, from Eastern Montana. He smokes his pipe next to the tripod that holds his sacred things. His dress reflects his spiritual creative-ness. For each item he has intimate feeling.

PIPE SMOKING

A pipe is an essential object for important functions. In the old days, every man had at least one smoking pipe, often the kind referred to as a "peace pipe." Most of the "peace" made while smoking such a pipe was inside the smoker's head. Such pipes sometimes had bowls that measured six inches or more, and stems that were two feet in length. These were smoked whenever friends and visitors gathered. Both men and women had small pipes, with stems hardly longer than a man's finger, for personal smoking.

Imagine, for instance, the experience of pipe smoking during the Vision Quest: Seated on a large boulder, way up on the side of a mountain; your Mind drifts High up into vast Space with the quickly diffusing smoke of each puff.

Imagine pipe smoking while sitting in a circle on the floor with a gathering of friends: All sharing of the same natural mixture; the mouthpiece giving lips a common bond and bringing to all a spiritual unity that is allowing only for Truth.

Pipe bowls used to be fashioned from clay or short pieces of hardwood, with reeds or hollow sticks used as stems. Some were drilled pieces of hard stone or Deer antler. The popular peace pipes are carved from a red stone called Catlinite. Some of these are still being made by Native craftsmen near the quarry at Pipestone, Minnesota.

In the Rocky Mountain country pipes of various shapes have long been carved from different-colored soft stones. One popular kind is a gray-green calcareous shale that is found along many streambeds. This kind was favored by the Blackfoot people. A square piece of stone, of the right proportions, must first be drilled for bowl and stem. The desired shape is then worked around the holes, first with a file, then with a knife and a piece of sandstone (or paper). The Blackfoot often made bowls in the shape of a large acorn resting in a rectangular base. For a final effect the finished bowls are held in the smoke of a brush-fire until they turn black. A coating of grease is then worked into each one to produce a lustrous black finish.

Pipestem holes used to be made by splitting a branch length-wise and scraping out the pithy center. The two sides were glued back together and wrapped with sinew (the muscle found along the backbone of large animals). Rosewood and Ash were preferred for stems. Holes can be made by using a straightened coat-hanger wire. Heat the wire in a fire and burn the hole straight through the stem. Partly dried Ash or Willow stems are best for this. Stems were carved, wrapped with beads, hung with bells and feathers, or just polished with fat to a natural finish.

A pipe used by the People of long ago can be easily made from the lower leg-bone of a Deer: The bone joints are sawed off. At the larger end is a cavity which may have to be scraped out--this will be the bowl. At the other end are two holes, which may have to be cleared out with a wire or nail--this will be the mouthpiece. Sand the

rough spots away from the edge of the bowl, and smooth the mouth-piece down to feel comfortable. Rub the now-completed pipe with fat and polish it. It is ready to smoke.

What does one smoke in a pipe when one lives with Nature? What-ever one becomes guided to, and can locate, is what! A popular social smoke in the past consisted of dry Bearberry leaves mixed with a little Cedar bark. Many times plants were especially raised and harvested, some times to the accompaniment of ceremonies. The seeds for such sacred plants (and smoking was always considered sacred) were carefully saved in decorated pouches, and were kept with Medicine items. The first plant was usually given as an offering to the Powers that gave life to the crop.

The dried and crushed plants for smoking should be kept sep-arate in decorated pouches. They are generally mixed just before smoking. Nature provides a great variety of blends.

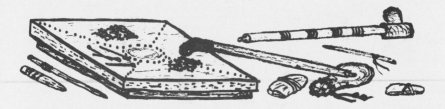

Most men kept a complete smoking kit in a leather bag. This kit included pipe bowls and stems, carved sticks to use for tampers and bowl cleaners, pouches of smoking mixtures, matches, and a cutting board. Cutting boards are the smokers' catch-alls. On them the smoking mixtures are cut and blended with a sharp knife.

A fine cutting board can be made using a piece of hardwood, about one foot square. Sometimes a smaller piece is fastened to the bottom, to give a table effect. In the top center is a depression, where the loose tobacco is mixed. The board is divided into four sections by lines made with brass furniture tacks. Brass tacks were a favorite item for decorating wood items, like pipe stems and gun stocks.

For smoking, the pipe is first lit, then offered to the spiritual world as a symbol of respect and awareness. The mouthpiece may be held out to the Four Directions, or to Sun, and the Spirits that are Above us, on Earth with us, and Below us. Some people blow whiffs of smoke to the sacred places, instead.

MR. & MRS. WADES-IN-THE-WATER ~ PIKUNI ~ INSIDE THEIR TIPI IN CEREMONIAL DRESS   GLACIER STUDIO

SWEAT BATHING

Sweat lodges were used by most native tribes. Many people today still take regular "sweats." The expulsion of dirt and germs through profuse sweating literally causes the removal of evil from the body. The plunge into cold water afterward serves to awaken both Mind and body. A "sweat" is a most profound spiritual experience--one that must be felt.

The sweat lodge is a small, round hut whose thick layer of coverings serves to keep the steam from heated rocks within. A typical sweat lodge is about eight feet deep and six feet wide.

To build a sweat lodge, clear a space big enough for the lodge. Locate the place for the door, which should face the rising Sun to the East. Dig a hole towards the rear of the lodge space for the rocks. This should be about two feet deep and two feet in diameter. Gather a quantity of flexible wood for the framework. Willow reeds, the thickness of a finger and ten to twenty feet long, are excellent. Working back from the doorway, plant the sticks firmly in the ground along both sides of the ground plan, perhaps a foot apart from each other. Tie together the ends of each pair of opposing sticks to form a series of arches. Allow enough head room for the number and size of intended bathers. Repeat this framework construction with the longer sticks arched from front to back. Remember to leave a door opening. Tie the arches together at intersections with buckskin thongs. Your framework should look like the neat beginnings for a gigantic basket, turned upside down.

Long ago, the Mountain People covered their sweat lodges with grass, or pine boughs, topped with firmly packed earth.

The People of the plains used Buffalo hides over theirs. The desert-dwellers of the SouthWest used adobe. Later, canvas and blankets were often used for coverings in place of native materials. Today, popular covering materials include quilts, rugs, and layers of carpet padding. Some lodge covers are more than a foot thick.

Lay your lodge coverings over the framework so that an oval opening remains at the entrance. The coverings must reach the ground and drape outward. In bright Sunlight the interior of the lodge should be totally dark, and free from air passages. Use a folded blanket, or several small floor mats, for the door flap. This should be held in place at the top by a couple of heavy stones.

Properly prepared, the first sweat bath is an experience always to remember. Mine took place on a cool Summer evening in a grove of trees at the foot of the Rockies in Western Montana. I was "initiated" by two friends whose life in Nature includes sweats most every evening--Summer and Winter.

Jerome and I sat on a wooden bench between two trees and un-braided our hair. Pascal was already taking red-hot stones out of the fire with a shovel and placing them in the pit inside the sweat lodge. The stones hissed defiantly whenever they came in contact with the cool, damp earth in there. Pascal says he looks for dark, smooth rocks in places away from river beds. These "sweat rocks" are about the size of a fist, and are heated on a bed of good firewood. (Where fire is a problem, about six pounds of briquets will heat rocks placed among them in a pit in two hours' time.)

We undressed and sat inside on a quilt-covered floor. When Pascal splashed water on the glowing rocks from a bucket, sounds like distant rifle fire filled our tiny chamber. Immediately we became enveloped by hot and heavy air. The steam was so thick, I thought I would suffocate. Jerome has been conditioned by more than fifty years of sweat bathing. He and Pascal, his nephew, took turns exclaiming the virtues of the "Good Sweat."

Three times we went outside for fresh air. The fourth time we went out singly to pour buckets-full of cold mountain water over our heads. I went out first, and passed out the second I stepped into the cold air. I fully dried and dressed myself before I again realized my physical location. I felt refreshed and hungry, as though I had just slept all night.

TIPI NOTES

A tipi is one of the most practical home styles ever made. Except for long poles, such a home can be compactly transported anywhere. Properly set up, it can house a dozen occupants comfortably-- cool in Summer, warm in Winter. You will want one after the first time you sit in one around a blazing fire with friends on a cold night-- or the first time you lay back on your bed, in one, and look up through the smoke-hole at a warm, star-filled Sky.

A 14-foot tipi is large enough to serve as a permanent home for a family of four. Drill, or unbleached muslin, make good tipi covers. The material should be hemmed wherever it is cut, and reinforced with rope inside the hem around the smoke flaps and door opening. The best poles are made from straight pine saplings, scraped and dried. The number and type of poles, however, depend mainly on the individual.

Most tipis were between ten and twenty feet in size. A ten-foot camping tipi can be easily made in one piece from a large canvas painter's drop cloth.

Painted tipis were rare. The one on the left in the photo illustrated its owner's war and hunting exploits. Other tipis had colorful representations of mountains, stars, and animals. These were all Medicine tipis, representing powerful Dreams. They should be respected as religious art, not copied or imitated for selfish reasons.

Tipi interiors are warmer and more colorful with the addition of dew cloths--six-foot-high linings of decorated canvas or colorful cloth tied to the inside of the poles all around the tipi. These serve to keep water from running down the poles, and to force upwards drafts from outside and smoke from within.

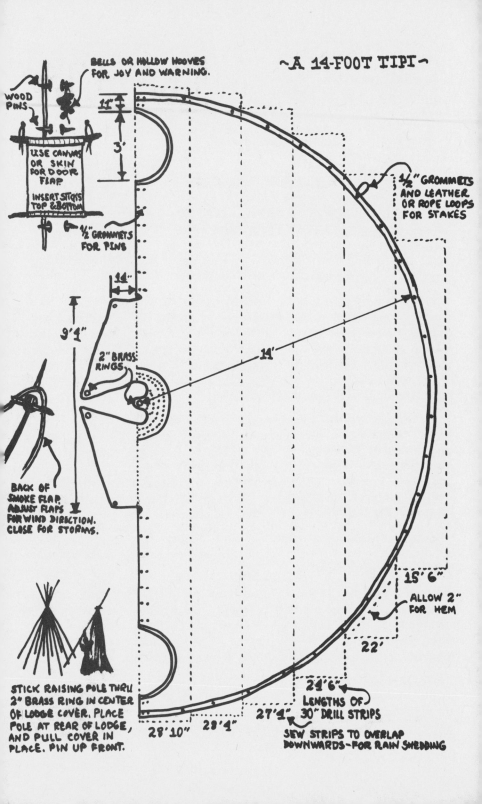

~A 14-FOOT TIPI~

BELLS OR HOLLOW HOOVES FOR JOY AND WARNING.

WOOD PINS

1"

3'

USE CANVAS OR SKIN FOR DOOR FLAP

INSERT STICKS TOP & BOTTOM

½" GROMMETS FOR PINS

½" GROMMETS AND LEATHER OR ROPE LOOPS FOR STAKES

14"

9'4"

2" BRASS RINGS

14'

BACK OF SMOKE FLAP. ADJUST FLAPS FOR WIND DIRECTION. CLOSE FOR STORMS.

15'6"

ALLOW 2" FOR HEM

22'

24'6"

LENGTHS OF 30" DRILL STRIPS

STICK RAISING POLE THRU 2" BRASS RING IN CENTER OF LODGE COVER. PLACE POLE AT REAR OF LODGE, AND PULL COVER IN PLACE. PIN UP FRONT.

28'10"   28'4"   27'1"

SEW STRIPS TO OVERLAP DOWNWARDS—FOR RAIN SHEDDING

OLD-TIME MOCCASINS

An old-time pair of moccasins is easy to make in one day. The effort is well worth the satisfaction of creating your own footwear. Soft buckskin is ideal for the tops. Untanned, or raw, hide wears well for soles. Thick Elk or Cow hide soles, however, are easier to sew. Split Cow hide can also be used for both tops and soles.

Begin by making a pattern as shown in figure 1, below. Trace your foot outline on a piece of paper. The pattern is cut slightly larger than the outline, as shown. This will allow the soles to mold upward around the feet. It will keep you from walking on the seam and wearing it out. Use the pattern to cut out your actual soles. Be sure to reverse for left and right. The grain side of the leather should be on the outside.

Use a large piece of paper to make the pattern for the uppers as shown in figure 2. Cut line A so that it measures 6 to 8 inches in length. Line B should be 2 to 3 inches wide to make the upper fit comfortably on your foot. Place the paper over your foot as in figure 3. Trace around the shape of your foot while pressing the paper to the floor. Add 1/8 inch around this tracing and cut out. Your upper pattern should look about like figure 4. Use this to cut your two uppers out of leather. Again, reverse for left and right.

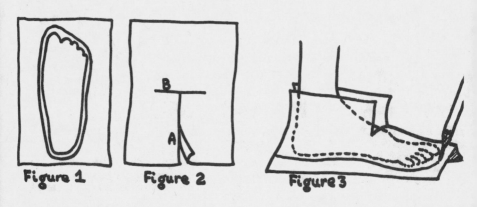

Figure 1   Figure 2   Figure 3

With an awl, make holes in the sole leather.   Space the holes 1/8 inch apart, and make them at an angle as shown in figure 5.   Place a sole and upper together and begin sewing the moccasin INSIDE OUT.   The needle should not come out on that surface of the sole which will eventually touch the ground.   As in figure 6, sew from the toe at C around one side to D, then from C around the other side to D.   Use an over hand stitch and well waxed nylon or other unbreakable thread.

When both moccasins are sewn up, turn them right side out. Wetting the soles will make this easier. Sew up the moccasin backs as in figure 7.   The flaps can be left standing, they can be folded and stitched down, or they can be extended with another piece of leather.   Add a tongue, and cut thongs as shown in figure 8.

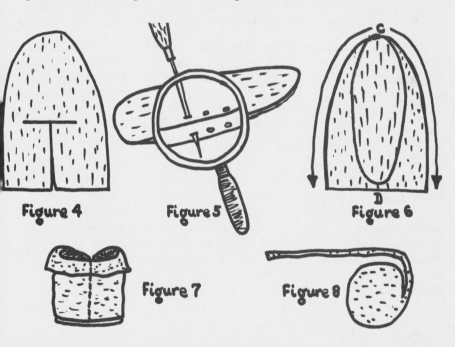

Figure 4   Figure 5   Figure 6

Figure 7   Figure 8

You now have a pair of Plains-style moccasins. This was the common footwear for people of the Plains, such as the Sioux and Cheyenne. It was well suited for their often-harsh country. It is today the most popular style of moccasin made.

For ceremonial wear moccasins were generally fully covered with beadwork.   Everyday moccasins were left plain, or decorated   with a beaded design on the toe. Winter moccasins were made of Buffalo hide with the fur left inside.

FUR CAPS

The caps worn by these two Blackfoot men are simple to make and comfortable to wear. Warmth and softness makes fur the most popular Winter headgear in cold climates.

On the right, old Black Plume is dressed for a Winter-time hunt, somewhere near his home by the Canadian Rockies. His cap is made of one piece of fur, sewn inside-out from the top of the front to the bottom of the back. The length of this piece is measured by holding it around the head the way it is to be worn. The height depends also on individual taste. The bottom of the cap is hemmed, and a cloth liner may be sewn to this hem.

The Pikuni leader Running Crane is seen dressed for battle. His Otter-fur cap is made in the two-piece style--a wide band sewn up the back, and a round piece sewn to the top. The main band can be hemmed at the bottom, or the fur may be doubled completely for extra warmth and strength.

Furs of all kinds, and even tanned birdskins, were used for caps. One's Medicine animal was often used for a cap, sometimes in a fashion that allowed the skin to be left intact. Dreams generally dictated any accessories that one might add to a completed cap.

Running Crane's style of shirt, incidentally, was worn on special occasions only, and represented dreams and accomplishments, in addition to skillful craftwork. When not being worn, these shirts were kept in rawhide containers, and treated as Medicine articles.

ONE-PIECE CAP

TWO-PIECE CAP

CABIN NOTES

"If you have built castles in the air, your work need not be lost. That is where they should be. Now put the foundations under them."

Henry David Thoreau

You can build a typical small frame cabin for about $250 if you live near a lumber mill. Such a cabin would have a solid door and a couple of windows, a wood floor, insulated walls and ceiling, and an attic for storage. There would be room inside for two beds, a wood-burning stove, a sink, some cupboards, and a small table. Additions could be made anytime later.

Log cabins can be built much cheaper than those made of milled lumber, if you have good trees on your property. The work is much harder, of course, and the logs take time to be seasoned. Log cabins are more difficult to heat and keep clean, and the chinking must be repaired regularly. The result of log cabin building is certainly an intimate home, as long as one has much more time than money. The house shown here is of a style which was popular among the Native People in the NorthWest country. Eight tree trunks were sunk in the ground to support the framework. Planks covered the outside, and an oval hole served as the doorway. The peak boards on the roof could be raised to draw out smoke and let in light.

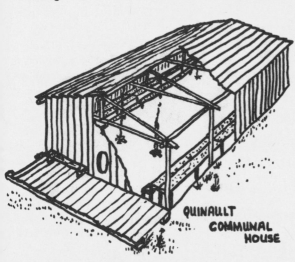

QUINAULT
COMMUNAL
HOUSE

Several families lived together in such houses, especially during the Winter. Sleeping platforms went around three walls inside. They were four feet wide and four feet from the ground. Sleeping is much warmer on this level than on the ground. Narrower platforms were built in front of the beds, two feet from the ground. These were used for seats and indoor work benches. In good weather the People preferred to work on the porch, outside.

BEADING

Beadwork decoration is a fine method for emphasizing pride in the design and workmanship of one's belongings. Beads vary in size from a pin-head to a pigeon egg, some rare types being even larger. After they became readily available from traders, the Native Americans used beads in countless different ways. With the tiny "seed" beads they developed a complex art form that was used to decorate clothing, tools, and even riding equipment. This art form was based on the ancient method of decorating by sewing down dyed and flattened porcupine quills.

Four methods of beadwork are commonly used. The easiest of these is done on a loom. A loom is easily made of wood, and should be about three inches wide and six inches longer than your planned beadwork. The tops of the upright pieces need grooves spaced 1/8 inch apart to hold the warp threads. Use heavy thread for the warp, and weave it back and forth across the loom and around the screws at each end, as shown in the drawing. Wax all thread with beeswax, to keep it from slipping.

LOOM BEADWORK

Head bands, belts, and hat bands are generally made on a loom. Plan the design on paper, and leave two warp threads on each side, for strength. Beads are strung on the weave thread, spaced across the warp threads, and pushed down to be passed through again by the weave thread below the warp. Begin in the middle and work towards the ends. Weave back and forth a few times to finish, and knot the warp threads together. Attach the completed bead strip to leather backing by sewing down the double-warp edges with strong thread.

More creative beadwork can be made with the "lazy stitch" method. Finished pieces done this way are distinctive for their ridged rows of somewhat loose beads. This produced an appearance that was especially popular among the People of the Plains. It was done by sewing several beads at a time directly to leather, these being attached only at the ends of rows.

Lazy stitch beadwork is generally applied directly to the item to be decorated. A knot is tied at the end of a waxed thread, and hidden on the reverse side of the beadwork. From two to more than ten beads are strung at a time and sewn down in parallel rows. The needle does not go entirely through the material, but catches only the outer edge of it. Figure A is a top view of the beads before being pulled tight. Figure B is a side view.

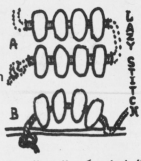

The third style of beadwork is known as the "appliqué stitch." Two threads are used, and every second or third bead is sewn down. This method produces the most perfect beadwork on leather. It is ideal for floral and pictoral designs. It was very popular among the People of the Rocky Mountain country, as well as the Woodlands People in the East.

The end of one thread is knotted and attached to the material. A number of beads are strung on it and laid in place. The second thread is then sewn across the first one, a stitch being taken at every second or third bead. Between stitches the second thread passes under the beads just below the surface, with leather. When bead-

APPLIQUE STITCH

ing on cloth the material must be backed for support, and the thread must be pulled all the way through. Beads may be sewn down in straight lines or in curves, as fits the design. Completed applique beadwork presents such a smooth, tight appearance that no threads are visible.

Circular pieces of beadwork are known as rosettes. They are often used where only a small amount of beadwork is desired--on leather vests, purses, and fur caps, for instance. They may range in size from a dime to a dinner plate.

Rosettes are generally made on backed felt or buckskin. Begin by drawing a circle on the material, and then draw in the design. Don't cut the circle out until you have done the beadwork. Knot the waxed thread, and sew down the center bead. Sew down the first row two beads at a time. Go back through the second bead again, each time. After

the first row, sew down four beads at a time, and go back through the last two. At the end of each row, run the thread through all the beads again, if they need to be evened up.

NATURE'S FOODS

If you are going to spend your time in Nature you should know the plants, animals, and berries that can be of direct food value to you. The best way to learn such things, of course, is to speak with an experienced outdoor person in your area. All men once "lived off the Land." You should be inspired to learn some of the knowledge which they have passed on to us.

As an example of Nature's foods, here is a short list of common plants that can be beneficial to you:

CATTAIL--Grows in moist and swampy areas. Boil or bake the roots and eat them like potatoes. Powder the roots and use for thickening soups. Use the shoots for salads--similar to cucumber. Mix the yellow pollen half and half with regular flour to make golden pancakes.

CRABGRASS---Gather the seeds and cook them like rice for a good breakfast cereal.

DANDELION---Grows anywhere, and is commonly eaten in many countries. Use the roots for tea. The white area at the top of the roots makes a good boiled vegetable. Leaves are good for salad or boiled greens.

MILKWEED---Eat the flowers raw, cook the shoots like asparagus.

NETTLES---Leaves can be boiled and eaten like spinach.

PURSLANE---Grows anywhere Gather whole plants and lay on sheet to dry in Sun. Then beat plants with stick to separate seeds, which make great pancake flour. Dried plants can be cooked in soups or stews. Fresh plants can be eaten as salad.

LAMB'S QUARTERS---Use young leaves for salads. Mix tiny black seeds in dough for nutrition.

THOUGHTS OF WISDOM

"That flowing water!
That flowing water!
My Mind wanders across it.
That broad water!
That broad water!
My Mind wanders across it.
That old age water!
That flowing water!
My Mind wanders across it."

Navajo Song of
the Old Age River

The Ancient Ones had no written literature to shed a light from the past upon their days of thoughtful search. Each had his own Way of Seeking Truths. If You are seeking, You have the opportunity of choosing from their many Ways. For NOW there is literature that tells us of Their Ways. Wise Men of many lands, many cultures, and many generations have left Us their Ways. They meant for us to use them. Their Words they meant for us to hear.

"Grandfather:
A Voice I am going to send!
Hear me,
All over the Universe:
A Voice I am going to send!
Hear me,
Grandfather:
I will Live!
I have said it."

Sioux Opening
Prayer of the
Sun Dance

Learn about the Ways of the Ancient Ones. Study literature and listen to Wise Men. Let the Old Ways help You to decide where you are going. Let the Old Ways help You to get there.

"Many Paths lead through the Forest,
But They All come out on the other Side."
OnistaiPoka

Think NOW of your Direction. Think NOW about your Path. Make your Trail meaningful--make every Step count. Don't stop to weep for those who would rather sleep. Stay Awake and Seek: from All that you meet.

"Often in my travels I come to the land of Spirits.
As day approaches I travel and come to the land of Spirits.
Often in my travels I come to the land of Spirits.
As Sun drops, I travel and come to the land of Spirits.
Often in my travels I come to the land of Spirits.
In my Dreams I travel and come to the land of Spirits.
Often in my travels I come to the land of Spirits.
As a Spirit I travel and come to the land of Spirits."

Osage Spirit Song

If you become lost, do not hesitate to take a new Path. Do not make a soft bed under a Bush, and there await your End. You may never know if the right Path is nearby. Do not let fear of the Unknown keep you from discovering the Unknown. Do not let discomforts keep you from finding more than comfort.

"The Old Men Say------The Earth only Endures.
You Spoke Truly------You are Right."

Sioux Song to overcome fear

Choose Surroundings of which you will want to speak well. Praise them often, in words and in songs. Find Good in All, and see that you replace it. Give, without expecting to take. But always Give, if You take. Goodness is Giving. Happiness is Giving. Giving is Goodness and Happiness.

"Footprints I make! I go to the field with eager haste.
Footprints I make! Amid rustling leaves I stand.
Footprints I make! Amid yellow blossoms I stand.
Footprints I make! I stand with exultant pride.
Footprints I make! I hasten homeward with a burden of Gladness.
Footprints I make! There is joy and gladness in my home.
Footprints I make! I stand amidst a day of contentment.

Osage Corn-Gatherers Song

It is the song of a content Mother who has brought home to her joyful family some of the fruits of her own labor. Her burden is a load of gladness.

.....AND ONLY TIME WILL TELL IF EACH GENERATION IS ABLE TO IMPROVE ITS LIFE WITH THE WISDOMS OF THE GENERATIONS BEFORE.....

COME TOGETHER

Where one man can survive, two will fare well;
Three and their Families will form a tribe.
A thousand like-Minds form their own Nation,
With Nature as the ruler of their Lives.

Brothers: Find Your Brothers!
Like Minds: Share Your Thoughts.
Let Customs and Traditions develop,
Let Respect be the Medium of Exchange.

Find Your Own piece of land to envelope,
Let Brotherhood of Your Minds grow along;
Love Your Brothers the way you love your own self;
Give Your children Paths to choose from that can't go wrong.

Come Together, Oh Brothers! Come Together,
Your Life on Earth is just so long;
Dig the Earth--know what comes of Your Digging,
Learn the simple Life of Nature--relax, let It Guide You along.

If Dreams of a Life of culture accompany Your desires for a home in Nature, then look for Companions. Seek others whose Dreams are like Yours. Get Together--give each other motivation. Get Together--Your ideas and resources. The results of Respectful coalitions will be seen in the strength of Your success.

Native People seldom traveled alone. They knew that Strength comes from Unity of Numbers. Families and friends camped together, hunted together, and defended together. The success of One meant success for All; none were left to suffer alone. Allegiance to the Group came before allegiance to self, thus the self was supported by the Group. With neighbors like Brothers, and Brothers for neighbors, no thoughts were kept hidden, no property hoarded. Generosity made a good man a leader; greed was the sign of discontent.

In the old days large groups of People, known as Tribes, seldom lived together in one body. The effect of such a mass on the Natural environment would have been unbearable to them. Water would have become polluted, forage would have been overgrazed, and game overhunted. Instead, smaller groups, known as Bands, were formed. These were People who were related (physically or spiritually--the Old People saw no difference), or who wished to follow the leadership of a successful man. New bands were formed regularly, and change of membership was not uncommon. And always: The bands could call on the rest of the Tribe in any case of need.

Leaders remained so only as long as they had followers. Band members remained so only as long as they put Group success before personal gain.

Bands of the same Tribe were often camped far apart from each other most of the year. Sometimes they only assembled once a year, for the great Summer Spiritual Gatherings which have been generally referred to as Sun Dances.

Sun is the ever-present symbol of the Great Power of All. When making a vow, in time of danger or need, Sun was often respectfully addressed as the Center of the Universe--the Great Power. Such vows were then often fulfilled during the sacred Sun Dances. Friends and relatives who lived with separate bands met and celebrated their continued Life on Earth together. Band leaders met and exchanged hunting and travelling information. Tribal leaders emerged as those whose actions and counselling were most sought after and admired by the People. The Sun Dance was the last opportunity for a great gathering of the tribe's bands before they set out in small groups to make preparations for the Winter.

What better time to gather in honor of Sun than in Summer, when Sun is nearest to the People who live all year beneath Its presence. At that time the trees are in full leaf, the berries are ripe, and the flowers are blooming--all with their faces to Sun in search of life and growth. At that time the weather is most pleasant, and the food is plenty.

And what great gatherings there were! Steady processions of People and Dogs arrived for days before the Sun Dance ceremony itself was to begin. Some groups traveled great distances to reach the Sacred Grounds. Many hundreds of tipis made up the tribal camp circles, each band having a space reserved for it by tradition. In the center of the circle was built the Sacred Lodge--the central point of the spiritual gathering. Nearby were the meeting-tipis of the various men's and women's societies, which furnished the police-men and attendants. A particularly large lodge in the center of camp served as the meeting place for the People's leaders.

Sun Dance ceremonies Naturally differed among the numerous tribes who performed them. The reasons for attending the cere-monies even varied among People of the same tribe. Some came to fulfill religious vows made during the year. Some came to ex-change spiritual knowledge and Medicine articles. Some came to show their abilities as spiritual leaders. Many came simply for the Spiritual Strengthening that resulted from the joyous gathering of so many like-Minds. Colorful clothing, tearful reunions, exchanges of presents, and happy singing were some of the common features of these gatherings.

To get an idea of the typical aspects of most Sun Dances let Us go back and visit a Dance of the Past. Let Us be with the Northern Cheyenne People, at their town of Lame Deer, Montana, around the turn of the century:

Multitudes of tipis and tents dot the Plain in a huge circle. Horses are seen grazing everywhere--singly and in herds. Buggies, buckboards, and covered wagons are parked by their owner's lodges, and show how households are easily transported. Outside a few lodges can still be seen travois poles, leaning against tipi sides like upside-down V's. The small cross-braces, to which loads are tied when the poles are being dragged by a horse, serve as steps for a handy camp ladder.

Hundreds of People are seen doing many things: visiting with each other; going to the river for Water, or a swim; hanging Meat over pole frames to dry; or beading a new pair of moccasins in the shade of a pine-branch Sun shelter. Others continue to arrive throughout the day, coming in various-sized groups and often from remote Villages on the Reservation. The arrival of such groups is often announced by their own young men, who charge into the huge camp circle on their horses, singing songs, yelling, and firing rifles into the Air. Some men ride into camps like this with their fraternal group, whose members all share some mark of identification, and who generally perform a few on-the-spot group songs and dances for the camp. All the new arrivals are dressed in their finest decorated clothes, and in just a short while their homes are set up and the fire is going.

As evening settles on the prairie the hundreds of fires light up the darkness. The air is filled with the smells of Cottonwood burning and meat cooking. The sounds of People talking and laughing are mixed with the sounds of drumming, as some sing their Spiritual songs and others meet in groups to practice lively tunes used for dances. It is a time for lighting pipes--for no good host would fail to offer his guests a smoke.

By the time the camp is completely set up the Leaders of the Sun Dance itself have already undergone some time of preparation: singing songs, sweat bathing and purifying, and preparing of the Sacred Articles to be used. A number of days might be spent before everyone is ready to concentrate on the Spiritual Experience of the Ceremony.

The first of the Four Important Days begins with the gathering of poles and branches for the Medicine Lodge.

This is done by men who are respected for their wisdom and courage, while the members of the Tribe look on. Old, respected men are then sent out to cut down a sturdy Cottonwood Tree, which will serve as the important Center Pole in the Medicine Lodge.

During construction of the Lodge, the Leaders of the Ceremony emerge from the preparation lodge and seat themselves on the ground near the new poles. There are three People who vowed during the past year to make this Summer's Sun Dance--they are called Pledgers. The wives of these Pledgers led the procession from the preparation lodge. Their bodies are painted according to custom, and they are wearing Buffalo robes wrapped around them. Bunches of fresh-smelling Sage are tied to their wrists and the sides of their heads.

The Pledgers are taken over to the partly-constructed Lodge to see the progress and to achieve Spiritual Communion by rubbing the poles with Sacred Red Earth Paint. Meanwhile, the women of the camp are given an opportunity to achieve Spiritual Communion with the Ceremony by bringing their children to the Sacred Women, who take each individual in their lap and say a prayer of Spiritual Strength for them. Presents are left before the Sacred Women by these callers in thanks for the hardships of fasting and self-sacrifice which these three Women are undergoing to aid the People with the Ceremony of Spiritual Strenthening. The Sacred Men, meanwhile, are looking on while sitting in a semi-circle to the right of the Women. Each of these Men was once a Pledger of the Sun Dance for his People.

Much shouting, shooting, and singing around the Center Pole, by all the People, is the signal of cheer that the Lodge is completed. The Sun Dance is now begun, and the People have given their approval. The Leaders of the Ceremony now enter to remain within the Lodge during the four days and nights of Ceremony.

That night, after dinner, comes the first assembly of the People to see the entrance of the Sun Dancers--mostly young men who have vowed to fast and dance for four days and nights in Spiritual recognition of some Powerful event which brought them Good during the year.

Older men, who have themselves once undergone the Sun Dance, accompany the Dancers and serve as Guides: giving the Dancers instructions, and painting their bodies. Drumming and singing accompanies the dancing for the whole time. At intervals all activity halts, the Dancers wrap themselves in blankets, and there is a period of rest. Most of the time, however, the Dancers face the Center Pole, look up toward Sun, and rise up and down on the balls of their feet in time to the drumming.

The Dancers are painted several times daily, and the designs are changed regularly during the days of the Ceremony. Clays, Earths, and Charcoal furnish most of the paint, which is then mixed with animal tallow for application. Breechclouts and waist wraps are the only clothing worn. In addition, each Dancer has wreaths of Sacred Sage on his head and wrists, and strung as a bandolier across one of his shoulders. Whistles of Eagle wing-bones hang suspended from each Dancer's neck. Fine Eagle plumes on their ends seem to float in air as the Dancers blow in unison to the drumbeats.

During one of the earlier rest periods in the dancing the Spiritual Leaders ceremonially construct the Altar of Life. This serves as a central place where those seeking Spiritual communion may go to pray and get strength. The center of the Altar is a Buffalo skull, with symbols of Nature painted on it. Around it are piles of dark Earth. Before it is a small pit for sweet-smelling incense, and an arch made of twigs to represent a Rainbow in the Sky. These are the things from the People's daily Lives.

A public feast follows completion of the Altar. Wagonloads of food are piled up in the Medicine Lodge, while the Spiritual Leaders make prayers of thanks for It All, and ask that the Good Spirit continue with the People.

All too soon the Great Summer Celebration is over. Homes are taken down and packed up. Groups of People head back out on the Prairie in All Directions. The events of the few days and nights will become topics of conversations during coming Fall and Winter campfires. The new Spiritual Strength will help Guide the next year's daily Life.

Housework in the days of tipi camps was a full-time job that often did not even allow for mistakes. The woman, in those days, usually owned the tipi and all the household goods, and was responsible for them. The husband was the provider and protector, but he often only watched when the tipi was being set up by the women, or when a new tipi was being made. The woman did all the cooking, tanning, sewing, and child-raising, as well as the firewood and berry gathering. Older children helped a great deal with this work, and many men had more than one wife to take care of all the housework. A wife's younger sisters, for instance, were often absorbed into the same household and generally made good companions this way.

The basic food item for most tipi-dwelling People was meat. On the plains, of course, this was primarily the meat of the Buffalo. In the mountains the meat was largely that of Deer, Elk, and Moose, supplemented by occasional Buffalo hunts out on the plains. Tipi-dwellers who lived by lakes and rivers learned to rely on Fish and Ducks, while some of the tribes on the prairies to the East even raised corn and other vegetables.

The best parts of an animal were often cooked over a fire and eaten as soon as possible. The Summer's heat and the constant travelling required preparation of the bulk of the meat so that it would not be subject to spoiling. Thus, most meat was dried by being cut into large, thin slices and hung out in Sun's light or

over a constant fire. Drying racks were made like the one pic-
tured above, or with a four pole foundation (like a topless table).
The four pole type can be covered with chicken wire for practical
regular use. Slice the meat into thin strips and slabs and lay
them across the wire or hang them from the poles. Some pieces
can be sliced in half again after they have dried and toughened a
bit. A smoky, almost - flameless, fire underneath will dry an immense quantity of meat, without burning, in a day or two. At
night the meat should be covered or taken inside to keep it from
getting moist.

The dried hunks of meat can be broken up and stored in large bags. It may be kept this way indefinitely, and eaten just as it is. It may also be toasted over a fire, fried in a skillet, or cooked with soups and stews. The same methods, incidentally, also apply to Fish.

Pemmican--the energy snack of the Outdoors--is made by pounding dried meat until it is fine and then mixing it with fat and berries. Hold the dry pieces briefly over the fire to make them soft and oily, then pound them with a heavy stone. Then heat some animal fat, bone marrow was particularly preferred, and mix it with the meat and crushed berries. A few leaves of wild peppermint were often added for flavoring. Five pounds of fresh meat will make one pound of Pemmican that can be divided and wrapped in small pouches to take on Winter hikes or hunting trips.

Here is how to make 10 pounds of Pemmican by the modern method: Take 5 pounds of dried meat and grind it until it has a meal-like consistency. Mix the ground-up meat with 1 pound of raisins (in place of berries) and ½ pound of brown sugar and then stir into 4 pounds of melted fat. Pemmican cakes were generally kept in rawhide bags, but canvas pouches will do. It may be eaten raw or fried.

Berry gathering was an important pursuit at Summer's end, in the old days. Bushes were often lightly beaten with sticks so that the berries would fall on robes spread out underneath. The robes were then taken back to camp and spread out again, so that the berries could dry in the Sunshine. Sometimes berries were spread out where the ground sloped, and a fire was built at the base to speed up the drying. Dried berries were stored whole and pulverized. Sometimes the fresh berries were mashed and pressed into cakes and then Sun dried. Several species were often mixed together for these berry cakes, which provided a nutritious change in fare during the long Winters.

SACRED TOBACCO CEREMONIES

Most Native People made a ceremony of the gathering of their smoking mixtures. They used the occasion to make known their wishes for success and happiness which they hoped would accompany their smoking times during the next Season. They prayed that Spiritual Awareness of the existing Powers should accompany their times of pipe smoking: while at home before the evening fire; while passing the pipe around a circle of friends gathered in the sweat lodge; or while blowing out whiffs of smoke to the Universe while seated on a rock outcropping far above the valley floor.

Certainly the time of harvest is a time to smoke in quiet contemplation of the Good Times Yet to Come! It is a wonderful occasion for singing songs and chants of the Montana region. For instance, tobacco planters among the Crow People used words like these in their songs:

> *"Tobacco is plenty, it is said,*
> *on the Mountain where I stay."*
> *and:*
> *"Some plants good---put on your heads."*

In the past an individual sometimes went out into the tobacco garden after the planting and spent the night there to seek a Vision.

An old-time Crow man named Gray Bull, in 1911, described an experience of this sort that he had had:

"I once lay at the garden for three days and nights. I slept. In the morning I got into water up to my breasts, faced upstream and downstream, and stayed all day until Sunset (Summer days in Crow country can be extremely hot). My body felt as though pricked. All my body was wrinkled up when I got out. I got out quickly and lay down in the shade. All my body felt as if pricked with needles. I lay down again by the garden and saw a man singing this song:

"I am Tobacco. My body all over is Tobacco."

At the first sentence he moved his clenched hand forward. At the second sentence he touched his body with it. After I got home I found my Tobacco growing very well, and I thought the song had something to do with it. The People asked me whether I had seen anything and I told them of my Vision. Then all said: 'Thanks! We shall surely have a good crop.' "

The Crow People developed a complex ritual for their Sacred Tobacco planting ceremony. The participants were members of the Crow Tobacco Society, whose ceremonial activities in the tribal life of the Crow were second in importance only to the Sun Dance. Members of the Society were trained for the respect and ceremony which was considered essential for the successful planting of the Sacred Tobacco.

CEREMONIAL MEETING OF CROW TOBACCO SOCIETY ON A SUMMER DAY

Members of the Tobacco Society "adopted" new members and taught them the pertinent songs and ceremonies. These new members thought of their adopters as Mother or Father in Spirit, and the adopters called them Children, in turn. Such Spiritual Relationships were generally life-long, and were no less important than physical relations. Children sought advice from their adopted Parents, and provided for them whenever the need arose. Presents were exchanged between the two whenever the situation seemed appropriate. A complex ceremony of adoption often took place inside an "adoption lodge." Songs were sung, gifts of appreciation were given by the new member, and Society Medicine objects were transferred to him by older members. The new member was shown ways to paint and dress at ceremonies.

The Blackfoot People raised their Smoking Plants in Sacred Gardens in which each family had its own plot. A band of the People would locate their Garden site and prepare it for planting in early Spring. The women and children helped to prepare the site. They removed debris, spread brush over the ground and burned it, and then swept the area clean with brush brooms. The soil was then broken up and raked fine by everyone present.

Tobacco Seeds were prepared by the Blackfoot for planting by being mixed with Elk, Deer, and Mountain Sheep droppings which had been pounded up. Sacred Serviceberries were then added to the mixture. Spiritual thoughts, songs, and prayers accompanied all phases of the planting ceremony.

The planters and their wives all met at the Garden on the actual day of planting. The planters stood before their own plots and then went across the field in a line, one step at a time. At each step they made holes in the ground before them with short, pointed sticks. Then the women followed behind and dropped some seed into the hole, and the Medicine Men sang one of the Tobacco Songs. This ceremony was repeated until the planting was done, at which time the Tobacco Dance was held. Then the People left the area of the Sacred Garden and went on their Summer hunts.

While the People were absent from the Sacred Garden they performed ceremonies at which prayers for the success of the crop were made. Some asked for protection of the crop from grasshoppers and other insects. While praying and singing they sometimes kept time with a stick, which they tapped on the ground as though they were killing these insects.

At harvest time the People all gathered and camped by the Garden again. The day before the Sacred Plants were gathered the wisest of the Medicine Men went to the Garden and brought back one plant. He then directed a young boy to take the plant to the center of camp. There he showed the boy how to fasten it ceremonially to a stick and leave it in the ground as an offering of appreciation to the Great Power which had caused the crop to grow successfully and to be ready now to Unite with the People.

On the day of the harvest a ceremony was held in the center of camp. A feast was served, prayers were offered, and songs were sung.....

"Sun goes with Us,"

were the words of one of the songs. The group of People then proceeded to the Garden and gathered their own plants. Fine pouches had been made and decorated prior to this, and these were now filled with the Sacred Plants to be smoked. Little decorated sacks were also on hand--these to preserve the precious seeds until the next Season's planting. The old-time Blackfoot People believed that these seeds were the ancestors of the first seeds given their forefathers of the long ago by a Medicine Beaver. The ceremonies of raising the Sacred Tobacco have, today, all but been forgotten.

THE GHOST DANCE:
SONGS & VISIONS

Father, I come;
Mother, I come;
Brother, I come;
Father, give us back our arrows.

......so went the continuous chant of the Sioux People as they gathered for the Ghost Dance--a spiritual revival ceremony in which the object was to lose consciousness of the physical state (which was at that time one which most People would not want to be conscious of)--a state of confined life on reservation land which seemed barren and desolate without the Buffalo herds and tipi camps that were everywhere a generation before. While under the spell of the Dance's excitement those who were fortunate fell to the ground in a trance and went on Spiritual Visits to places of beauty--visiting the camps and People of another day.

The history and anthropology of the Ghost Dance has been well described in several books. Let us see here about some of the Dance's spiritual methods. Ghost Dance leaders among different tribes patterned details of the ceremony to compliment traditions that already existed within their own tribes. Styles of dress and types of songs, for instance, were common tribal variations in Ghost Dance Ceremonies.

......As We join an Arapaho Ghost Dance camp of the past We find ourselves in the midst of almost 100 tipis. The People have located the Camp in a grove of tall Cottonwood trees next to a little river. It is late in the afternoon, and the People are putting on beaded clothing and combing their hair in preparation for the Dance.

Some wear only aprons--they are painting elaborate designs all over their bodies with red, yellow, green, and blue mixtures of sacred paints. Red and yellow paint lines the parting in their hair. Dots like hailstones are seen on some faces. Sun, stars, crescents, crosses, and birds are seen on bodies. Others have these designs painted on white clothing.

The Dance leaders of the camp are the first to assemble around a tree which marks the very center of the dance area. They hold hands and quietly begin singing this song:

> Eyehe'! na'nisa'na,
> Eyehe'! na'nisa'na,
> Hi'na cha'sa' aticha' ni'na He'eye'!
> Hi'na cha'sa' aticha' ni'na He'eye'!
> Na'hani na'nitha'tuhu'na He'eye'!
> Na'hani na'nitha'tuhu'na He'eye'!
> Bi'taa'wu' da'naa'bana'wa He'eye'!
> Bi'taa'wu' da'naa'bana'wa He'eye'!

In English the song says:

> O, my Children!   O, my Children!
> Here is another of your pipes---He'eye'!
> Here is another of your pipes---He'eye'!
> Look!   thus I shouted---He'eye'!
> Look!   thus I shouted---He'eye'!
> When I moved the Earth---He'eye'!
> When I moved the Earth---He'eye'!

The song is sung a number of times and it grows in strength, as voices become louder and others join in. The dancing starts slowly to the left, in rhythm with the singing--right feet shuffling after left. The People of the camp join in with the handholding, shuffling, and singing until All become a part of a sacred, revolving Circle of men, women, children, and Old People. The Mass becomes a gigantic Vibration.

No one notices that evening is slowly coming on. Some of the dancers have unclasped their hands and are sitting on the ground smoking and talking. Others are beginning to shake noticeably from the intensity of the spiritual feeling.

From within the ring advances one of the spiritual leaders, dancing in unison with the group, but facing a Young Man who is shaking. The leader is wearing a cotton apron and a white flannel shirt with many birds and insects drawn upon it. His hair hangs loosely over his

shoulders and he holds a black and white Eagle feather in his left
hand, a red scarf in his right. He twirls first the feather, then the
scarf in front of the Young Man's face, all the while muttering a low
Hu! Hu! Hu! Hu! The words of the song that fills the now-night
air are: "Na' nanu' naatani'na Hu'hu!" Soon the Young Man loses
his place in the dance circle as he looks at the hankerchief and Eagle
feather--or looks through them to the beginnings of his Vision beyond. Having the Young Man's full attention the Older keeps him
spellbound by waving the feather swiftly, then slowly, then twirling
it, then fanning his hands in the air, then in front of the Young
Man's face, then, finally, drawing his hands from in front of the
Young Man's eyes, slowly up into the Star-filled Sky, until the Young
Man stops shaking, becomes rigid, and falls to the Earth to go to his
Vision. The Experience of the Older has brought the Youth from his
state of physical hopelessness to a state of Spiritual Ecstasy whose
moments of delight and happiness are worth the hours of daily toil++++

The other dancers continue, and the leader moves on to another
person. Everyone is careful not to disturb those who are having Vi-
sions--carefully dancing around them where they lay on the Earth.
These Dreamers often stay gone for several hours.

It is supposed that the popular Ghost Shirts originated in a Dancer's Vision some time ago. On the white background the owners of these shirts paint sacred symbols representing Nature, and illustrating some aspect of a Vision they have had. While Dancing, the Shirt is worn as an outside garment by many men, women, and children. Many, in the Past, wore it underneath their daily garments at all times. They believed that the Shirts gave them exceptional Power.

Ghost Shirts are made of white buckskin, whenever this is obtainable. Most of the Shirts are made of white muslin, and are sewn with sinew instead of thread. The sleeves, shoulders, and necks of the Shirts generally have extra strips of cloth sewn between the seams, and this is cut into fringe. Eagle feathers are often attached to the shoulders and sleeves. The designs are generally applied with colored paints, but some of the fine buckskin shirts and dresses of the Past were completely decorated with beadwork. Some Shirts have only a few designs on them, while others are completely covered with Sun, Moon, Stars, and other Natural symbols.

Most Ghost Dancers of the Past were antagonized into believing that going beyond physical reality to seek spiritual experiences was evil. Yet, the doctrine of Wovoka--the Ghost Dance messiah of the Past--is still believed by some to describe one of the Paths that lead to Happiness:

> "You must not fight. Do no harm to anyone.
> Do Right always."

MORE GHOST DANCE SONGS

> Verily, I have given you my strength,
> Says the Father, Says the Father.
> The shirt will cause you to live,
> Says the Father, Says the Father.
>
> Sioux Ghost Shirt Song

> My Children - E' e' Ye'!
> My Children - E' e' Ye'!
> Here it is, I hand it to You.
> The Earth - E' e' Ye'!
> The Earth - E' e' Ye'!
>
> Arapaho

> I love my children - Ye' ye'!
> I love my children - Ye' ye'!
> You shall grow to be a nation - Ye' ye'!
> You shall grow to be a nation - Ye' ye'!
> Says the Father, says the Father.
> Ha ye' ye' Eya' yo'! Haye' ye' Eya' yo' yo'!
>
> Sioux

> I Fly around yellow,
> I Fly around yellow,
> I Fly with the wild rose on my head,
> I Fly with the wild rose on my head,
> On high - He' e' e'!
> On high - He' e' e'!
>
> Arapaho

ON NAMING PERSONS

Names of many Native American Persons are well known for their color and beauty. The stories behind such names are often even more colorful and beautiful, for many such names originated in Visions or were given as a permanent reminder of some notable event

Methods of name-giving varied among the many tribes. Most individuals, however, had more than one name, and some changed their name a number of times during their life-time. A given name at Birth, and an earned name for adulthood was the most common system by which Persons were named.

The parents of a newborn child generally called some respected old person to their lodge to give the baby a name. This person would ask if a particular name was preferred--one Dreamed of by the parents or, perhaps, one that was asked to be passed on by some relative. If not, the old person might give the child the name of some animal or other Natural Being whose presence was noted at the time of the Birth Or, the old person might previously have Dreamed of a name to be given to the next child that needed one. Or, the person might pick out a name or event from his or her own past with which to honor the child. It was quite common for an old warrior to name a baby girl for some battle exploit of his. Names such as Two Strike Woman and Night Horse were carried by women of the past.

An event during childhood often brought a new name to an individual. Sometimes this became the life-long name, at other times it represented an embarrassing aspect in the person's life. Such names as Lazy Boy, Round Head, and Sits Like A Woman were life-long names of the past. If the individual showed dislike for the commonly-given nickname he might find the name turned into "Not Want to be Called Lazy Boy."

Upon reaching adulthood an individual could take on a new name by several means, such as through Dreams. Sometimes a person who was in the midst of accomplishing some brave deed would choose a new name and shout it aloud for all to hear. Or, again, an outstanding event might be condensed into a name by which the person became popularly known.

Names given to the People of the past were of a much greater variety than the common "White Eagle" and "Morning Star" of cinema fame. Two word names were often abbreviations of names that made complete statements. Thus, a man known as Eagle Walker might actually be named "Walks as quietly as an Eagle flies." Inventory Clerks for last century's Leaders of Manifest Destiny were often the first ones to "officially" record the names of Native tribe members--names that were then applied permanently to the offsprings of these members. Generally these names were given in their short forms by the obliging People, and were then translated into suitable words for ledgers.

Among many tribes it was considered respectful not to ask a person his name, or the origin of it, lest he be forced to draw unwanted attention upon himself or his Spiritual beliefs. Some old-time People, in fact, never spoke their own name for that reason. Other individuals, however, were publicly proud of their names and had pictographic signatures by which they were known. Below here, for instance, are the "signatures" of a few of the followers of the old Sioux chief Red Cloud. When the government agent "chose" a new chief for the tribe, Red Cloud's People showed their opposition through a petition of several paper sheets of these signatures. These were sent to Washington, D.C., where they were, no doubt, respectfully received.

SMOKING BEAR   SCRATCH·THE·BELLY   GOOD BIRD

LEAVES   LITTLE BEAR   OLD HORSE   EAGLE HORSE

WOLF·ON·A·HILL   CHARGE AFTER   HIGH BEAR

"Peaceful People" means Hopi--far and wide reaches the Earth around them: Why quarrel with another about the distance of the far-ness, or the method to cross the width? Let each one wear the moccasins he makes for himself--let him choose the Paths to wear them.

Far and wide is the Earth around the Hopi: with no signs of trees--no signs of Water. OMNIPRESENT is the Desert to the Hopi: to them, the Earth. Spiritual Strength is in everything known to the Hopi: how else could anything survive in their World? Why little hidden places of Water--there in the trackless sands? Why little groves of trees--there between the barren ridgetops? Why little crumbling catacombs--built by the Ancients there on the Sunburnt mesas? Why All these things: if no Great Spirit were to draw them together?

For more than 800 years have the Hopi centered their lives around several little villages built separately on distant desert-hill-tops. For all those centuries have the People of that tribe lived their totally-Spiritual lives: leaving little offerings at their few gathering places of water, to demonstrate their thankfulness for even that amount; having ceremonies to pay their respect to Sun, and give thanks for the *good* done by Sun for them; singing songs of praise to the hardy little plants of corn and squash that thrive in the sand of the Desert to give the People most of their food.

Sometimes feeling miserable even with shade and Water, the stranger in the Land of the Hopi questions the availability of anything but sand and heat. Yet, the Hopi have learned that everything in the Nature of the Great Spirit was intended to harmonize together. So it is that the Hopi cherish all the Natural elements that let them go on living: the cultivated Maize, Beans, Squash, Watermelons, Peaches, and Sunflowers; the Salt, brought ceremoniously from waters far away; the Clays, dug from remote hillsides and packed home for the making of utensils; and the hunted Coyote, Rabbits, Prairie Dogs, Rats, Hawks, Owls, and Foxes, taken home for their sparse meat and their furs, feathers, and bones.

Farming has always been a struggle with the elements of Nature for the Hopi: hot Sunshine and no Rain; or Rainstorms to wash away seeds and destroy tender, young plants; or Hailstorms to smash mature plants before harvest; or Windstorms to tear up plants and smother gardens in knee-deep sand; or weeds to drain the precious moisture and strangle growing crops; and, of course, a variety of small animals and insects who, like the Hopi, have to make use of everything they can find in order to subsist in the Desert.

Can You fail to succeed finding Spiritual Happiness, no matter what your conditions, with the knowledge that the Hopi People have been succeeding for centuries? Is it not ample proof of the strength of a Natural Spiritual Life?

The Hopi have usually started their first crops in April. Sweet Corn is at that time planted in holes dug four inches deep, the seeds being covered by two inches of soil. Mice, rats, and worms have never lost any time in searching for the seeds, and often the whole crop has had to be replanted. Windbreaks are made around the holes with small twigs and pieces of brush. Tin cans, opened at both ends, have been used in later days, for they also cut down on animal damage.

Other crops are planted according to the condition of the Weather. Melons, Squash, and Beans are usually in by the end of April. Muskmelons, Watermelons, and Lima Beans are planted in May. The Melons are planted in sandy soil, and the hills are placed five steps apart. By the middle of June most planting is completed with a final crop of Corn--the main staple of the Hopi People.

Corn planting has often been done co-operatively by several men. Holes are dug 6 to 9 inches deep, and several feet apart, with Greasewood planting sticks. 12 to 15 grains of Corn are dropped into each hole. The resulting clumps of Corn plants are easier to keep moist than long rows. The plants are fertilized--a common old-time mixture was composed of dried roots, dung, and pulverized parts of animals, which was mixed with water and sprayed on the plants.

Stakes are used to mark the location of crops, as sandstorms regularly cover all signs of planting. Dirt is packed tightly around the plants, once they come up, to help keep worms away from the roots. And to avoid offending the Corn Maiden Spirits, who spiritually protect the crops, Hopi farmers have been careful not to have intercourse with a woman in the cornfields.

Harvested Corn is brought home, shucked, and left to dry on the roofs of the houses. It is then stored indoors in bins--the People being always careful to keep enough on hand to take care of a whole Season's crop failure. The dried Corn is ground to make the popular, crispy-thin Piki bread. It is also ground into corn flour, corn mush, corn bread, and hominy. The husks are used to make a Hopi tamale. And the stalks are ground and fed to the livestock.

The many spiritual dances and ceremonies held by the Hopi throughout the Seasons are all tributes to Earth fertility and life-giving Rain, and to the Spirits who share these Benefits. Out on the Desert, across the centers of the Villages, and down in the underground Kivas are sung the songs and said the prayers that give to the Hopi a spiritual meaning for everything in Life.

BROTHERS: FIND YOUR BROTHERS . . . . . .

. . . . LET COMPANIONSHIP MAKE
LIGHT THE BURDENS IN LIFE. . . . .

"WHERE THERE IS A WILL THERE IS A WAY"—IF YOU PRAY

If we will assume that the words "Will" and "Mind" can be interchanged, then we find ourselves saying, in effect, that "the Mind is everything." If You can clear your Mind of all but good things, then your desires will all be good; your ways to those desires will be good—Your life will be Good! But how to clear the Mind of all but good things?

Decide that goodness in Life is all you want—and You can clear Your Mind of all but goodness. I say this not from a righteous throne—I confess to having other-than-good thoughts much too often (for my Mind's desires). I am only too well aware that the Way may come much later than the Will. The paycheck often comes much later than the work—for those who are on that path. The Harvest, after all, is not expected to be on the same day as the Planting. Plant in your

Mind the desire for good thoughts—water that desire with inspiration, regularly—weed it objectively—and convince Yourself (as countless others have, now and then—as I have) that the Harvest time will come, and you will reap a lifetime supply of good thoughts. Your desires should be able to preserve them quite well—even through stormy weather.

How do you plant, in Your Mind, the desire for good thoughts? Well, that depends upon the Path which you are following. If we use the term prayer very liberally, then I would suggest praying as the finest way to turn your Mind towards good thoughts. And how to pray? Well, well, now—if we haven't just touched upon a hot topic for debate. Or have we? That's what you can often hear: "Never argue about religion, because there is no end to the argument," says some critics. Keeping good thoughts in Mind, I'll disagree with that. Here is what I say:

Do YOU think your religion is right? Does it make YOU happy? Does it keep YOU from trespassing against others? Yes? Then, brother or sister, you have found the right religion for YOU!

What difference is it to me how Your religion balances out on the scale of mine? If it doesn't belong on there, then I won't put it on there—then it won't affect the balance of mine, eh? Now, if You will accept all that, then there won't even be a beginning for an argument about our methods of prayer—we'll just say to each other: "Yours is good. . . .Yours is good."

And what if you don't accept my suggestion of "what's good for you and doesn't hurt me is good"? Well, I'll show you my garden; give you a sample of the harvest; hope I've inspired you; and let you go back to survey the extent of your own weed patch. If you still like it, then that's good, too. Just give me a little respect. . . .

Now, back to planting that garden of desires to have only good thoughts—planting through praying. From various things that I've said—today and at other times—You've probably gathered that my Mind is very much inspired by the Spiritual Powers that have long inspired Native People who spent their whole lives with the Nature of this North American Land. I'm inspired by the sight of Birds and Animals—the climbing of Mountains—the smell of Flowers and Trees—the feeling of Wind and Rain—the falling of Snow—I'm inspired by living with these things; I'm inspired by mentioning them in my prayers—they remind me of the many things in the Universe that flow so beautifully together in Harmony with Nature. I'm inspired to know—to make myself aware that I am just like All those things—a part of Nature—able to flow beautifully if I make an effort to live in Harmony with Nature—my brothers and sisters.

Since thinking of All these good things during my prayers is so inspirational to having, always, good thoughts, it follows that the more I pray the more I will be inspiring myself to have good thoughts—the more good thoughts I will have. If You can't comprehend what I'm saying, then I beg You to try it—try praying in such a way as to mention those things that exist (anywhere in the

Universe) and that inspire you to have good thoughts. Do it through whatever form of prayer you think is right for you—loudly or meditatively. Better yet, try several forms—try loudly and meditatively. Remember: it's not the method of praying that counts—it's the thoughts that You have while praying.

And don't think that I'm suggesting You will find happiness in life by giving lip service to some "prayers." A bunch of words falling from your mouth won't make the weeds in your garden disappear. Do your praying with your Mind! Let your mouth help, if you want, by saying words and singing songs that inspire good thoughts to enter your Mind. But don't let Your prayers come only from your mouth. For we all know where *that's* at, eh?

If you make a regular effort at praying—by thinking good thoughts—and you live in an environment that makes you happy, then You will soon find that many of the things you do in your daily life give you good thoughts and can, thus, add strength to your prayers. Your prayers can involve more and more of daily life—by spending more and more of your time doing those things that are good enough to pray about—until You (and I, says my Mind) find yourself doing only those things good enough to pray about—and then all the goodness will make Your Life a Prayer.

A NIGHT-TIME CEREMONY ON THE PRAIRIE

All day the People have rested—tonight is the Ceremony of Holy Smoking—tonight the People will stay up all night to sing and talk and eat and to say prayers of strength with the smoking of their pipes. Tonight will be a holy night.

Late afternoon is here now: see the coming of darkness—see it as it covers up the last shades of orange over the mountains in the Western sky. Darkness comes soon up on these Northern Plains, during these cold days of early Winter.

In their houses the People who are going to the ceremony tonight are now getting themselves ready—inside their houses that dot the Prairie here and there; some are surrounded by a sheltering growth of trees and bushes; some are nestled under a bluff by the side of a river; but most of them sit out on the open Plains—like tiny landmarks announcing the presence of People amid the vastness of the Universe—on top of endless Earth and underneath all-covering Sky.

Now lights come on inside the houses—yellow glowing through framed glass windows: some diffused by sheets of plastic protecting windows from the Winter storms soon to come. Horses and cattle graze near by different ones. A large Owl sits somewhere in a tree, hooting softly, in the now-almost-darkness in the yard of one of the houses. A bunch of dogs bark and play, by another. A voice is heard singing, from a third one—the tune can be heard across the Plain:

> . . . Man, he says, my tipi is powerful.
> Woman, she says, my tipi is powerful.
> Rain is my Medicine.
> My children, they hear me.
> The Earth, it is powerful.

The chant goes on—the words are only a small part of it—the chanter can be seen inside his little house, moving around in a room lit by one bare light bulb. He is picking up things here and there: the wood stem and stone bowl for a large smoking pipe, which he puts in a paper bag; a small buckskin pouch of tobacco, and the old woolen cap, which goes on his head. Nearby him, his old wife sits in a chair, re-braiding her hair—she wears one of her long, print-cloth dresses. She sings the song too, for she knows it as well. It belonged to their long-ago Medicine tipi. At the ceremony they will sing it again—remembering when—and hearing the others sing like songs. Out on the Prairie, around them, in the chilled air of evening goes the song:

> . . . Man, he says, the water is our home.
> Woman, she says, the water is our home.
> Water, is my Medicine.
> My tipi, it is powerful.
> My tipi, it is powerful.
> Woman, my tipi, it is powerful.
> I mean it, my tipi, it is powerful. . . .

Some while after full-dark comes, the People begin to arrive for the ceremony—not many will come, for not many have TIME now! Few, today, see the vastness of the Spirit that is with Us all the time. But those few—well, tonight they will gather: to help each other make themselves remain aware. Some of them come to see more than others—but they must see, at all, to even be there.

Few come in cars—few here have them: young relatives and others drop them off. The drivers halt momentarily to leave the old ones, before they hurry away from they-know-not-where. In the house by the coulee the old ones gather, to be with All the Spirits who will be there.

A few young ones have come to the ceremony—a few young ones who know some Spirit they will find There. They come, and the old ones are happy, thinking: "Sad, so few, but at least some will be here."

A hush of respect greets the Old One—though on canes and nearly blind, he's like a Bear: Sacred Earth on his face—sacred bearing—Sacred Earth adding red streaks to long, white-grey hair. Coming inside, towards the back he moves—slowly but surely: taking the place of honor, for the leader must sit there. His couch: an old, folded robe of Buffalo bull; his shoulders draped and covered by a blanket; and on his moccasins: a flower, beaded there.

Before the Old One: an altar—a box of dirt to represent our Earth Mother—a small pipe inside it, lying there. To each side of the Old One sit the others—on cushions, for the room is cleared bare.

With a prayer, the Old One starts the ceremony: "Hiyo Spirits, we're gathered with You here. Hiyo Old Ones, Hiyo Medicines, Hiyo All of You Powers, hear our prayers, hear our songs that we sing for You. Be with Us, give Us guidance everywhere."

With prayers and songs, the Old One fixes the sacraments—some Sage leaves and Sacred Earth to remind Us of the Spirit of Prairie Life. As each one takes the sacrament, he says words of goodness and asks for blessings from the Spirits that only He knows are There.

Around goes the sacrament: to young and old—each one says a prayer, short or long. A helper brings a hot coal from the fire, with a forked stick he carries it to the altar. The Old One sings a song, brings forth his incense, puts some Sweetgrass on the coal that's lying there.

The night is long—soon some food is brought to help the physical discomfort that All must bear. Wooden bowls filled with meat and rolls—cups of tea—many apples; the talk is good—the food fills up bodies—Minds think of prayers.

Into paper bags goes the surplus food—carefully saved to be eaten at later times—when the ceremony will only be a strength-giving memory during the cold Winter days and nights. Outside goes one old man with his apples, putting on a fur cap before opening the door. In comes a cold draft—causing some to pull tighter their coats and blankets. Outside: to his team of Horses walks the old man with his apples—over to where they are standing beside each other; an old, green-painted wooden wagon hitched on behind. A few words of comfort he mutters to his Horses, that old man, and from his hand he gives them each an apple. Then he comes back inside and sits down—the others, too, are again settling in their places.

The attendant brings another coal from the fire—more Sweetgrass is placed on the coal—again, the air becomes pungent; again, the songs and prayers begin.

Now, a man goes outside: out into the dark, cold air to bring in a large object from its quiet, sacred place of resting. The object represents the Spirits who are with the gathering this night—things fastened to it are symbols that help everyone present to think of the powers of the Universe: Eagle Plumes to tell Us of the Birds and the Sky; fur to tell Us of the Animals and the Ground; Sage to tell Us of the Earth and the power of growth; crossed sticks to tell Us of the four directions and the powers which come from them; other symbols, too, with holy meanings to those present. More prayers are said—prayers inspired by the symbols of the powers known to be present.

The Old One sings a song:

"Sacred Paint, I am looking for it."

He reaches into a sack of things and brings out some old buckskin bags, while he's singing the words,

"Sacred paint, I have found it. It is holy."

He lays the buckskin bags of sacred paint before him. He brings out a piece of cloth in which is wrapped a small chunk of fat. Like a bar of soap, he rubs the chunk of fat between his palms until his hands are coated with a greasy layer. Carefully, he feels of the buckskin bags—his sight is too dim to let him see them well—he feels of them until he is content that he has found the right one. He unties its buckskin thong, opens up the bag, and dips two of his fingers inside: into the powdered mass of Sacred red Earth. Chanting all the while, he mixes the red Earth into the grease on his hands until his hands are thickly coated with shiny red. Then begins the ceremony of the painting.

Those who desire to be annointed with the Sacred Earth—those who feel that the annointing, done by the Old One, will later bring them memories to inspire strength when needed—they take turns going up before him, kneeling down, looking into the Old One's already red-painted face, hearing up close his songs and prayers of good wishes, and feeling his greasy, gnarled, old hands rubbing the Sacred Earth across their foreheads, over cheeks and chins, around the wrists, and over their hair. Thus painted, each one turns his back, still kneeling, and receives the Old One's blessing as he passes the Holy Symbol of the Universe over their heads and bodies.

When it is finished—the ceremony of painting—a pause is taken to allow everyone time to prepare for the next part of the ceremony.

Outside, the night is clear and cold—Stars twinkle brightly—and a fine ring of orange surrounds Night Light's bright, full body like a thick circle of Sacred Paint. Nostrils tingle with each breath as the still, cold air freezes the moisture inside them. Each one hurries quickly back, and through the doorway—back to the cozy warmth, by the old wood stove, that waits in there. Only one comes back slowly—feeling no more the need to hurry—his body worn—his Mind strong, for the speed of his presence: no care.

Again seated on the floor around the room is the gathering—sacred things, and the altar, in their midst. Some light talk, making pleasant the gatherers: some laughter, some good memories in the air. Cups of tea, held by hands slowly rewarming. Says the Old One: "What foolishness, this; drinking warmth to fight cold caused by drinking so much warmness—like wiping dust from the wiper of dust! Still, he drinks, like the others, the warm liquid; he drinks the tea among the gathering, there.

Half the night is over, when begins that part of the ceremony in which All participate, and each devotes. For now comes songs, and smoking pipes, and holy prayers; and words of courage passed on from ancestors, for Us to hear.

Next to the altar are stacked the smoking pipes of the partakers—each has his own, among the pile that's resting there. One of the helpers dumps out the herb, from sacks used while smoking; he dumps it out, in a pile, on the cutting board. With a knife, he cuts the herb—mixes it up to prepare it for smoking; fills the pipes—one by one—that are lying there. One of the Old Men takes each pipe and says a prayer, holds it over—in sacred way—the smudge of incense. In sacred way each helper then takes them—to have some Old Ones light them up and say more prayers.

Around go the pipes—each one smoking—each one blowing sacred wisps out in the air. Before long, it is finished, all this smoking. Before long, begin the songs of those gathered there.

First, the Old One gets out four sacred rattles, from the bag of things he has brought along. Buffalo rawhide, sacred painted, are these rattles, in time with singing, they will be shaken by those who hold them, by those who tap them on scarves laid down before them. But not until the Old One has held them over the smudge of incense—in sacred way—has prayed in time to sacred shakings of them. Not until then are the rattles placed in the hands of those who will first use them.

Tsht-tsht-tsht-tsht . . . goes the rhythmic sound of the four rattles as the holy singing begins. The men take turns singing four songs each—the women in background accompany them. Each one tells the meaning of his singing—from where the song came—what sacrifice was made to obtain the song, and the spiritual article it came with. All those present are aware of the powers of what's described there—of the songs and ceremonies that are represented there. Many have owned the same items, in the past once, as have their forefathers who are mentioned—strong as their presence that we all feel, gathered there.

Tsht-tsht-tsht-tsht . . . on goes the rattling and singing, the pipe smoking, the incense burning. On goes the night. Many are the songs sung—many are the Spirits thereby represented. As each one knows the sacrifice and devotions that the different songs are representing, none would consider singing any songs but those to which he is entitled—though all might help with the singing of the different songs of the devoted. Only one young man in the group joins the singing—at this time he is the only one who is devoted enough to the Spirits present to make sacrifices for their help—to learn their songs and ceremonies. From his sacred bundle he sings the words:

"It is powerful, this sweetness, take some of it.
I use it for a sacred purpose. . . .
. . . There he comes, Old Man.
He is walking this way.
He is coming in.
Come in with safety.
'Let us have a sweat,' he says . . .

. . . Old Man he says:
'My old smoke, I do not feel it.'
Old Man, he says:
'My new smoke, I feel it.'
It is powerful. . . .

. . . Now then, that which is above:
He knows me.
It is powerful.
This here, that which is below:
He knows me.
It is powerful.

As the night goes on, more food is served. Afterwards, the singing continues as does the praying, the talking, the smoking, the spiritual thinking . . . on and on and on and on . . . till finally comes the first sign of dawn—a thin, light line separating dark, starlit Sky from horizon. The singing is finished, the pipes are smoked out, done are the prayers, happy is the crowd. A last meal is provided: sacred blood soup cooked with sacred tongue. Like our ancestors have always done before Us, so we take a piece of tongue and hold it up—let our Minds dwell on the Spirits represented—say our prayers of good wishes for everyone. After eating, at last, goes out the Old One—soon we won't see his presence any longer—but his Spirit will be with Us everywhere.

The Breath of one who prays to his spirits while crossing a frozen lake with his Dog-team in the far North joins the Breaths of others like him up there—joins their Breaths and those of the Walrus and Polar Bear—the Seal and the Reindeer—all those Breaths joining and coming South—coming in a Sacred Way to bring those who are South some of the Spirit of the Life of their Northern Brothers. And So it is with the People far to the South—sitting in dugout canoes while floating on tropical waters, searching for the day's meal—their Breaths of prayer joining those of the Ocelot and Iguana—the Parrot and Llama—bringing to those of the cooler North some of the Spirit of the Life of their Southern Brothers. From East and West, also, come the Breaths of Brothers elsewhere. From the Earth—our Mother—come the powers of growth and strength—comes the Spirit of the Life of our long-gone Brothers, whose Earthly beings and belongings have become, again, a part of our Mother. And from Above come the powers of light and guidance—the Spirit of the Life of the Above Ones—Sun, Moon, Stars, and Sky; all the unseen others who live up on High.

See Them, Brothers—join Them. Let their Breaths give your thoughts cause to cry. Cry from happiness—knowing All who go where you go—send your prayers with Your Breaths to join the Sky.

SMOHALLA AND HIS DREAMER PEOPLE

Along the Columbia River, in what is now the state of Washington, there once lived a religious leader whom you will be interested to read about. His name was Smohalla, which means "The Preacher." Many of his people, however, called him by another name—Yu'yunipi'tquana—The Shouting Mountain, for a mountain spoke to him during some of his religious dreams, which he had while sleeping on that mountain.

Smohalla was a warrior and religious leader as early as the 1850's among his Wanapum People, and for a few members of the neighboring and related Yakima Tribe. Around 1860, however, he was involved in a fight with another leader, from a nearby camp, who left Smohalla lying on the ground for dead. Smohalla disappeared, and for several years the 200 or so People of his tribe saw nothing of him, assumed he was dead, and mourned for him.

Somehow, Smohalla had managed to drag himself down to the river and into a canoe, in which he floated off with the current and towards the Pacific Coast. In those years, during his absence from his People, he traveled all over the West, physically. Spiritually, he also went a long way.

When he came back to his own People he brought with him the spiritual beliefs and ceremonies that had most inspired his thoughts among the different People with whom he had visited. To his People he was like Jesus—one that had been resurrected. They expressed their happiness for his return by their dedication and enthusiasm for the new Spirits he had brought along.

This is the way Smohalla described, for his followers, the meaning of Life:

"Once the World was all Water, and God lived alone. He was lonesome, he had no place to put his foot, so he scratched the sand up from the bottom and made the land, and he made the rocks, and he made the trees, and he made a man; and the man had wings and could go anywhere. The man was lonesome, and God made a woman. They ate fish from the water, and God made the Deer and other Animals, and He sent the man to hunt and told the woman to cook the meat and to dress the skins. Many more men and women grew up, and they lived on the banks of the great River whose banks were full of Salmon. The mountains contained much game and there were Buffalo on the Plains. There were so many People that the stronger ones sometimes oppressed the weak and drove them from the best fisheries, which they claimed as their own. They fought and nearly all were killed, and their bones are to be seen in the hills yet. God was very angry at this, and He took away their wings and commanded that the lands and fisheries should be common to All who lived upon them; that they were never to be marked off or divided, but that the People should enjoy the fruits that God planted in the land, and the animals that lived upon it, and the fishes in the water. God said He was the Father and the Earth was the Mother of Mankind; that Nature was The Law; that the animals, and fish, and plants obeyed Nature, and that man only was sinful. This is the old law."

"After a while, when God is ready, He will drive away all the people except those who have obeyed his laws," predicted Smohalla.

Regarding the new arrivals in his country, he said:

"They ask me to plow the ground! Shall I take a knife and tear my mother's bosom? Then when I die she will not take me to her bosom to rest.

"They ask me to dig for stone! Shall I dig under her skin for her bones? Then when I die I will not enter her body to be born again.

"They ask me to cut grass and make hay and sell it, and be rich like white men! But how dare I cut off my mother's hair?

"I want my people to stay with me here. All the dead men will come to life again. Their Spirits will come to their bodies again. We must wait here in the homes of our fathers and be ready to meet them in the bosom of our mother."

Upon his return, Smohalla urged his People to avoid most of the newly-arrived "civilization." Instead, he promoted a strict tribal life of fishing, hunting, gathering, and praying—a simple and natural life that he felt would bring for All the most in spiritual happiness.

In keeping with the spiritual feelings brought to the People by others, Smohalla proclaimed Sunday as a day for only holy matters. On that day he gathered with his People for morning, afternoon, and evening services. Any day, however, services were likely to be held, and anytime at all was right for the saying of prayers.

Smohalla's popularity, of course, was not happily accepted by those who were coming to "establish" laws which were not necessarily in Harmony with Nature. One of their representatives—a Captain E. L. Huggins, of the second Cavalry, reported the following conversations with Smohalla. The righteous captain conversed with his mouth open and his mind closed.

"Smohalla: 'My young men shall never work. Men who work cannot dream, and wisdom comes to us in dreams.'

"Captain: When it was argued that the whites worked and yet knew more than the Indians [quantity vs. quality, eh, Captain!], he replied that the white man's wisdom was poor and weak and of no value to Indians, who must learn the highest wisdom from dreams and from participating in the Dreamer ceremonies. Being pressed to explain the nature of his higher knowledge, he replied:

"Smohalla: 'Each one must learn for himself the highest wisdom. It cannot be taught. You have the wisdom of your race. Be content.'

"Captain: I contended that even the Indians had to work hard during the fishing season to get food for Winter.

"Smohalla: 'This work lasts only for a few weeks. Besides, it is natural work and does them no harm. But the work of the white man hardens soul and body. Nor is it right to tear up and mutilate the Earth as white men do.'

"Captain: I asserted that the Indians also dug roots and were even then digging camas in the mountains.

"Smohalla: 'We simply take the gifts that are freely offered. We no more harm the Earth than would an infant's fingers harm its mother's breast. But the white man tears up large tracts of land, runs deep ditches, cuts down forests, and changes the whole face of the Earth. You know very well this is not right. Every honest man [said Smohalla, while looking at the captain searchingly] knows in his heart that this is all wrong. But the white men are so greedy they do not consider these things.' "

Smohalla's beliefs and efforts inspired numerous Native groups along the Columbia River to follow his example. Religious ceremonies that combined Native with Biblical teachings gave much spiritual uplift to many People whose lives towards "civilization" had been filled with despair. One of Smohalla's disciples was a Yakima by the name of Kotai'aqan (Scattering Ducklings). A Major Mac Murray visited with this disciple, pointing out that he was "pacific and gentle." Said MacMurray:

"He said all men were as brothers to him and he hoped all would dwell together. He had been told that white and black and all other kinds of men originally dwelt in tents . . . and that God in former times came to commune with white men. He thought there could be only one Saghalee Tyee, in which case white and red men would live on a common plane. We came from one source of life and in time would Grow from one stem again. It would be like a stick that the white held by one end and the Indians by the other until it was broken, and it would be made again into one stick."

Major MacMurray spent some time visiting at the camp of Smohalla, at Priest Rapids on the Columbia. Parts of his report from there help to give us a picture of Smohalla's People and their spiritual lives. He says:

"We reached the plain and were met by a procession, headed by Smohalla in person, all attired in gorgeous array and mounted on their best chargers. We wended our way through sagebrush and sand dunes to the village street, not a soul being visible, but from the mat-roofed Salmon houses there came forth the

most indescribable chorus of bell ringing, drum beating, and screeching [?]. I noticed that the street was neatly swept and well sprinkled. . . . Our procession passed on beyond the village to a new canvas tent, which had a brush shade to keep off the Sun and was lined and carpeted with new and very pretty matting. Smohalla said this had been prepared especially for me . . . he had constructed a bench for me, having sent more than 90 miles for the nails. Fresh Salmon . . . were regularly furnished my party. . . . The River was within two yards of our tent door and was an ample lavatory [Indeed! I hope they caught your fish downstream from there, Major!]

"When I awoke the next morning, the sound of drums was again heard, and for days it continued. I do not remember that there was any intermission except for a few minutes at a time. . . .

"There was a small open space to the North of the larger house, which was Smohalla's residence and the village assembly room as well. This space was enclosed by a whitewashed fence made of boards which had drifted down the river. In the middle was a flagstaff with a rectangular flag. . . . Smohalla explained: 'This is my flag, and it represents the world. God told me to look after my people—All are my people. There are four ways in the world—North and South and East and West. I have been all those ways. This is the center. I live here. The red spot is my heart—everybody can see it. The yellow grass grows everywhere around this place. The green mountains are far away and all around the world. There is only water beyond, salt water. The blue is the sky, and the star is the North Star. . . .

"There are frequent services, a sort of processional around the outside of the fence, the prophet and a small boy with a bell entering the enclosure, where, after hoisting the flag, he delivers a sort of sermon. . . .

"This house was built with a framework of stout logs placed upright in the ground and roofed over with brush, or with canvas in rainy weather. The sides consisted of bark and rush matting. It was about 75 feet long by 25 feet wide. Singing and drumming had been going on for some time when I arrived. The air resounded with the voices of hundreds of Indians, male and female, and the banging of drums. Within, the room was dimly lighted. Smoke curled from a fire on the floor at the farther end and pervaded the atmosphere. The ceiling was hung with hundreds of Salmon, split and drying in the smoke.

"The scene was a strange one. On either side of the room was a row of twelve women standing erect with arms crossed and hands extended, with finger-tips at the shoulders. They kept time to the drums and their voices by balancing on the balls of their feet and tapping with their heels on the floor, repetition wore them out, and I heard that others than Smohalla had seen visions in their trances, but I saw none who would admit it or explain anything of it [to a cavalry major, I probably wouldn't either].

"Those on the right hand were dressed in garments of a red color with an attempt at uniformity. Those on the left wore costumes of white buckskin, said to be very ancient ceremonial costumes, with red and blue trimmings. All wore large round silver plates or such other glittering ornaments as they possessed. A canvas covered the floor and on it knelt the men and boys in lines of seven. Each seven, as a rule, had shirts of the same color. The tallest were in front, the size diminishing regularly to the rear. Children and ancient hags [forgive me, grand-mothers—I'm only repeating the Major's words!] filled in any spare space. In front on a mattress knelt Smohalla, his left hand covering his heart. On his right was the boy bell ringer in similar posture. Smohalla wore a white garment which he was pleased to call a priest's gown, but it was simply a white cloth shirt with a colored stripe down the back [the major wore a blue outfit, which he was pleased to call a soldier's uniform, but it was simply a blue cloth coat and trous-ers with colored stripes on the arms and legs].

"Smohalla's son was said to be in training as his successor. He was a young man, apparently about 23 years old, tall, slender, and active in movement, and commonly kept himself apart from the body of the People. He ordinarily wore a short gown of surplice, sometimes yellow and other times sky blue, with ornate decorations of stars or moon applique cut from bright-colored cloths. The sleeves were extravagantly trimmed with beads and silver ornaments."

While busy noting technical details, the Major may have missed a few basic points. The ceremony performed by Smohalla and his People was a group effort at Spiritual unity and awareness. The combinations of songs, prayers, bells, and drums, with the physical involvement and personal beauty that the participants strived for brought about an immense Spirit that was only their version of the religious experience that has been sought and found by many. The group goal is spiritual unity—the individual goal is of ecstasy during which individual mem-bers often experienced their Minds passing out of their bodies. Upon their return, and during various breaks in the ceremonies, these individuals would recite their visions and experiences to their brothers and sisters. Every factor was another color in the picture of spiritual happiness sought by ALL.

I am happy to tell you that a number of descendants of Smohalla's follow-ers still fill their lives with his methods of prayer and devotion. Here and there, in the Columbia River country, People still dress in their finery and gather to the sound of bells and prayers and chants—gather for the inspiration that they re-ceive from the spiritual sessions and the holy feasts of water, salmon, and berries which always follow. It is well.

A STORY OF LIFE

FROM THE SIOUX PEOPLE

Wazi was chief of the People who dwell under the world, and his woman, Kanka, was a seer. Their daughter, Ite, the wife of Tate, was the most beautiful of women. She gave birth to four sons at one time, which proved these children to be gods. Yet Wazi was not content, for he wished to have powers like a god. Iktomi knew this and he schemed to have Wazi play his pranks. He told Wazi that he should have the powers he wished for if he would help make others ridiculous. Wazi was afraid, but he told Kanka what Iktomi had said. She said that if they had the power of the gods no one could take it from them and then they could laugh at Iktomi. Iktomi, lurking near, heard her say this, and smiled.

He went and sat in the tipi of Kanka. He told her that she was a wise woman and a seer and that for a long time he had thought she ought to have power to do as she liked. He said he would be pleased if he could help her get such power so she could do much good for the People. He then talked of the beauty of her daughter, Ite. He said that because of her beauty she was the wife of a god and the mother of gods and therefore ought to have a seat with the gods. He talked much like this. Kanka asked him how he could help her get power to do as she wished to do. He said he would think about this and then tell her.

When Iktomi had gone, Wazi told Kanka that if she was not careful Iktomi would make the People laugh at her. Again, Iktomi came and told Kanka that if she would help him play his pranks he would give her power to do as the gods do. Kanka said that if he would first give her and Wazi such powers and they could prove that they had them, then they would help him to do what he wished. Iktomi agreed to this and gave them the powers they wished for. Then he talked of the beauty of their daughter until the night was almost gone.

Early the next morning he came and told Wazi and Kanka that they could prove their powers by making anyone more beautiful. He showed them how to make a charm that would make more beautiful anyone who would carry it on the body. He then went to the tipi of Ite and sat and talked with her. He told her that she was very industrious and modest, that she was as beautiful as Hanwi, and that if she were more beautiful she would be the most beautiful of all human beings.

Ite told her mother what Iktomi had said and Kanka told her that she would sit with the gods. Again, Iktomi sat and talked with Ite. He told her that Wi, the chief of the gods, had noticed her beauty and had spoken of it. Again, Ite told her mother what Iktomi had said, and Kanka said that Ite would sit with the chief of the gods. She gave her daughter the charm and bade her carry it on her body. Ite carried the charm and grew more beautiful each night. Iktomi told Wi that the wife of Tate was the most beautiful of all beings, that she was the wife of a god and the mother of gods, and that she ought to have a seat with the gods. He then sat and talked with Kanka and told her that it would please Wi to see Ite.

Wazi told Kanka to be careful or Iktomi would cause the People to laugh at her. She said that they could laugh at Iktomi, for he could not take from them the power he had given them; that when the People that now lived were forgotten, People would speak of Wazi and Kanka because their daughter sat with the chiefs of the gods. Iktomi lurked near and heard her say this and he smiled.

Ite adorned herself, but there was no fire in her tipi, neither was there food nor drink, and her little sons cried because they were hungry. She walked with her father and mother, and they passed before the face of Wi. Wi saw that Ite was very beautiful and then he remembered what Iktomi had said to him. So he talked with her and invited her to sit at the feast of the gods.

Iktomi sat in the tipi of Ite and talked with her. He told her that Wi was tired of his companion, Hanwi, and wished for a younger and a more beautiful companion. Then Ite told him that Wi had invited her to sit at the feast of the gods. He told her that when all were seated at the feast, she must take the vacant seat. Kanka helped her daughter to adorn herself and foretold that Ite would live forever like the gods.

When the feast was ready, Iktomi was talking with Hanwi. He told her that Wi thought that a woman, Ite, was the most beautiful of all beings and had invited her to sit at the feast of the gods. So Hanwi stayed to adorn herself and came late to the feast. Ite came early and when all were seated, she saw a vacant seat beside Wi, and she took it. Wi did not frown. He smiled and talked with Ite. Hanwi came and saw a woman sitting in her seat. She covered her head with her robe and stood behind Ite. The People saw this, and they laughed at her. Iktomi laughed loudest and longest. Kanka sang a song of joy, but Wazi was afraid. Tate left the feast and went to the tipi of Ite. He painted his face and the faces of his little sons black.

After the feast, Hanwi stood before Skan hiding her face with her robe. Skan asked her why she hid her face. She replied because she was shamed by Wi who had permitted a woman to sit in her place so the People laughed at her and Iktomi laughed loudest and longest.

Then Skan asked Wi why he had permitted a woman to sit on the seat of Hanwi. Wi replied that because of the beauty of the woman he had forgotten his companion Hanwi.

Skan asked Ite why she sat on the seat of Hanwi. She replied that her mother foretold that she would sit beside the chief of the gods and had made her more beautiful, that Iktomi had told her that she was the most beautiful of all beings, that Wi was tired of Hanwi and wished for a younger and more beautiful companion, and that Wi invited her to sit at the feast of the gods, that she had seen the vacant seat beside him and sat on it.

Skan asked Kanka why she had schemed to have her daughter sit on the seat of Hanwi. She replied that as a seer she foresaw that Ite would sit beside the chief of the gods, and that she and Wazi had gotten from Iktomi the powers to do as the gods do. By these powers they had made their daughter more beautiful, so that Wi would not be ashamed of her when she sat beside him, and that Iktomi had told her that Wi was pleased to see Ite.

Skan asked Wazi why he had gotten the power from Iktomi. He replied that he wished for the power so that he could do more good.

Then Skan told Wi that the gods must not forget; that because he had permitted the beauty of a woman to cause him to forget his companion, she would be his companion no more, that she could go her own way and travel as she pleased; that he and she had ruled the two periods of time, day and night, but that forever after she would rule the third period, the interval between the time she went from him until she returned to him; that because he had caused her to hide her face for shame she would forever hide her face when near him, and only uncover it when she was far from him.

Skan told Ite that because she had forgotten her husband and little sons she would be with them no more; that her unborn child would come before its time and it would forever be a little child and abide with Tate; that because she was so vain of her beauty that she dared try to usurp the place of Hanwi, she would go to the world and there live forever without friends; that she should keep her beautiful face forever, but she would have another face so horrid that those who looked upon it would fly from her or go mad; and that she would be known as Anog Ite, the Double-Woman, or the Two-Faced.

Skan told Kanka that because she had obtained the power of a god by fraud she should go to the world and there live alone forever, until she could use her powers to help little children and young people, and that she would forever be known as Wakanka, the Old Woman, the Witch.

Skan told Wazi that because he had not used his powers to do good, but to cause shame for his kindred and the gods, he should live forever alone in the world until he could use his powers to help his grandsons and that he should forever be known as Wazi, the Old Man, the Wizard.

Then Iktomi laughed loud and long and taunted Wakanka and said that she would have cheated him to get the powers of a god and then would have laughed at him, but that he had made her and her kindred ashamed.

Skan then asked Iktomi why he had schemed to make Wakanka and her kindred ashamed and to cause shame for Hanwi. Iktomi said that he was a god and the son of a god, that his father, the rock, was the oldest of the gods, that he had named all things that are named and made all languages that are spoken, that he had done much good and should be treated as a god; but because his other parent, the flying god, had no shape, his form was queer and all laughed at him; that when he did good all laughed at him as if he were making sport, that because everyone laughed at him he would laugh at everyone; that he had made the chief of the gods and the most beautiful of the gods ashamed; that he had made the chief of the People and the most beautiful of women ashamed; and that he would make all the gods and all the People ashamed.

Then Skan told him that because he laughed when others were ashamed or suffered and because he threatened the gods, he must go to the world and remain there forever without friends; that all of mankind would hate him, and all the gods despise him, and that the sound of the rattles would be torture to him.

Then Iktomi laughed loud and long. Skan asked him why he laughed. He replied that Skan had forgotten the birds and the beasts; that he would dwell with them and talk with each in its own language, and that he would have pleasure and would make fools of mankind.

Then Tate blackened his face and with his four sons sat before Skan. Skan called him his comrade and asked him what he wished. Tate told Skan to look upon his face and the faces of his little children that were blackened because their mother was taken from them forever. He said Ite was but a woman and that others stronger than she had caused her to forget the woman's place; that though his sons were gods, they were little children and wept for their mother's care. He begged Skan to let him bear his punishment of Ite and let her remain with her children.

Skan told Tate that because of his love for Anog Ite, he would dwell near her until the fourth period of time and then he could do with the woman as he wished, that he could send a token to Tate and then Tate would send four sons to establish the directions on the world and they would make the fourth period of time.

Hanwi blackened her face and mourned with Tate, and the People laughed at her no more.

Before the directions were given to the world, Tate with his four sons and his little son dwelt in his round lodge beyond the region of the pines. At midday the Sun looked through the door of the lodge toward the place of honor to see that all was well with Tate. The seat of Tate was the place of honor and that of his oldest son, Yata, was beside him. The seat of the second-born, Eya, was at the right side of the lodge, and that of the third-born son, Yampa, was at the left side, while that of the youngest son, Okaga, was beside the door. His little son, Yum, had no birth; therefore, he had no seat in the lodge, but sat where he chose.

Tate did the woman's work in the lodge. Each morning his four sons set out to travel over the world. Sometimes Yum traveled with Okaga. One time when all the sons were away, something shining fell near the lodge, and Tate went to look at it. It was a woman wearing a soft white dress. She carried a queer pouch that was marked with strange symbols. He asked her whence she came, and she said she came from the stars. He asked her whither she would go. She replied her father had sent her to find friends on the earth. He asked who was her father; she replied that the Sky was her father. Then Tate told her to come with him to live in his lodge. He bade her tell his sons nothing of who she was or whence she came. He gave her the woman's seat in the lodge. When he began to make a robe of tanned skin, she said she would do the woman's work in the lodge and so he gave her the skin.

She took from her pouch a sharp stone and cut the skin into queer patterns. Then she took from her pouch an awl and sinew thread and quickly sewed the pieces together and made a garment which she gave to Tate and showed him how to wear it.

In the evening, Yata came striding to the door and jerked the flap aside and looked inside the lodge. He saw the woman and then he gazed at his father. He went away from the lodge and sat and stared at the ground. Soon Eya came, singing and hallowing, and threw the flap up and looked inside the lodge. He saw the woman and his father; he looked from one to the other and sat beside Yata and gazed at the ground. Then Yanpa strolled up to the lodge and raised the flap and started to go in, when he saw the woman. He looked at her and then at his father, and then at the lodge inside and out. Then he went and sat with Yata and Eya and he, too, gazed at the ground.

Soon Okaga and Yum came back together. Okaga asked his brothers why they sat and gazed at the ground. Yata said that the witch was in the lodge; Eya said that their father was wearing a strange garment; and Yanpa said there was nothing to eat. Yum ran to the door and lifted the flap and saw the woman. She looked at him and smiled, and he went inside the lodge. She bade him to sit beside her. He sat down and continued to gaze at her eyes. She put her arm around him and he smiled at her. Okaga came to the door and saw Yum sitting beside the woman and smiling at her, so he went inside. He saw that the woman was young and beautiful and that her braided hair was long and smooth, and her dress was white and clean and that even her feet were clothed. He sat at his seat. Then Tate remarked that he had forgotten his work, and it would be late before he could prepare the food for the evening. The woman offered to prepare the food. Immediately there was a fire in the fireplace and there were hot stones in it. She put the stones in the cooking bag and the food boiled. Then she told Tate that the food was ready to be served. Okaga gazed at her, astonished, but Tate only smiled as if he were well pleased.

He called his sons who were outside to come and eat. Yanpa said that there was no food prepared when he looked in the lodge. Eya said that no one had brought wood or water and the food could not be ready. Yata was sure it was the witch who had bewitched their father and the food. Again, Tate called. Yanpa consented to go in. He sat at his place and stared at the woman. Yata said, "She will bewitch him also." Eya said, "The witch was old, but this woman is young." Again Tate called. This time Eya said that this was but a young woman and he would go inside. He went in and sat at his place and stared at her. Then Tate called again, saying that the food was prepared and they were waiting for Yata so that they might eat. Yata said, "She is the witch, but I will drive her from the lodge." He strode to the door and stepped into the lodge, scowling. The woman looked at him and smiled. He gazed at her and then meekly went to his place and sat down. He looked around the lodge, at his father and at little Yum who sat beside the woman. When the four brothers were seated, all silently gazed at the ground though Yum continued to gaze at the woman's eyes. Tate gazed at the fire and smiled as if something pleased him.

Then the woman asked Tate what he most wished to eat. He replied he would like tripe and wild turnips and soup. She took from her pouch a new wooden bowl and platter and from the cooking bag tripe and boiled turnips, and she dipped the bowl full of soup from it. She gave these to Tate and called him her father. The brothers all looked at her and then at their father, but he only gazed at the fire and smiled. Then she called Yata her brother, and asked him what he most wished to eat. He said he wished boiled flesh and fat and pemmican and soup. She took from her pouch a new bowl and platter of wood, and from the cooking bag, boiled flesh and fat, and she dipped from it the bowl full of soup, and she placed pemmican on the platter and gave it all to Yata. Then she called Eya her brother, and asked him what he wished to eat. He told her he wanted a boiled Duck and wild rice and soup. Again, she took a platter and bowl from her pouch, and from the bag a Duck and rice and placed them on a platter, and dipped the bowl full of soup and gave them to Eya. Then she called Yanpa her brother, and asked him what he wished. He said he wanted tripe, flesh, fat, a Duck, turnips, rice and soup. She put all these things on a platter and in the bowl that she took from her pouch and gave them to Yanpa. Then she took from her pouch a little platter and a little bowl. On the platter she put strange food and in the bowl strange drink that had an odor of sweetgrass. She handed these to Yum and told him to give them to his brother who sat by the door. He did so. Then Yata said that as he was the oldest of the brothers, she should give him the best food instead of to the youngest. Okaga looked at the food—there was little of it—he looked at the drink and there was little of that. Then he looked at the woman, but she and Yum were eating together. He put all the food in his mouth and it made only one mouthful. He ate it and it was good. He looked at the little platter and there was more food on it. This he ate and still there was more food on the platter. He drank all there was in the bowl and immediately it was full again. So he ate and drank until he was satisfied.

When it was time to lie down to sleep, the four brothers went out of the lodge and found a new tipi nearby. They lifted the door flap, and inside they saw four beds, one at the place of honor, one on the right, one on the left side and one near the door. Yata said it must be the witch. Eya said the witch had treated them well. Yanpa said he wished the witch would always prepare their food. Then the three brothers went inside the tipi. Each lay on his bed to sleep, but Okaga sat beside the water, and played on his flute. The music was as soft as a whisper, but the woman heard it, and she smiled. Yum asked her why she smiled, and she said because he was always to be her little brother. Far into the night, Okaga sat by the water and gazed at the stars.

In the morning Okaga rose early as was his wont, to bring wood and water for his father; but when he came to the door of the lodge he found much wood and the water bag was full. The fire burned with hot stones in it and the cooking bag had food in it. The woman was astir but she did not look at Okaga. The father called his sons and all came and each sat in his place. The woman served them with food, and it was good. When all had eaten, the father told his sons that the time appointed by the Great Spirit was completed, and now there would be a fourth period of time. First, he told them, they must fix the directions of the world, but when they returned to his lodge, it would be the fourth period; that since they were four brothers, they should fix a direction for each of them, and thus there would be four directions; that they should go to the trail around the edge of the World and travel together until they came to the place for each direction, and there they should pile a great heap of stones to mark the direction forever. He said Yata was the oldest son and entitled to the first direction, which must be where the Sun goes over the Mountains and down under the World when his day's journey is done. The direction for Yanpa must be where the Sun comes up by the edge of the World to begin his daily journey. The direction for Okaga must be under the Sun at midday. He told them that the journey must be long, that it would be some Moons before they returned to his lodge, and that there would be as many Moons in the fourth time as had passed from the time they left the lodge until their return. He told them to prepare for four days and start on their journey on the fifth day.

For four days they prepared; on the morning of the fifth day they went from their father's lodge. When they had gone, Tate mourned for them as for the dead, for he knew they would abide in his lodge no more.

The wizard was not permitted on the world, so he traveled around on the edge until he made a trail there. He spoke to the Stars as they passed near him and asked each for permission to go to the World, but they never granted his request. He saw that some Stars never came down to the edge of the World, so he set up a lodge under them and dwelt in it so that he might be near if they should come down, for he thought one of them might give him permission to go on the world. In this lodge a vision came to him in which he was told to go on the trail again where a message would come to him. He followed the trail around the edge of the world and a bright star spoke to him. It appeared in the form of a beautiful young woman, who told him she was the daughter of the Sky and that her father had sent her with a message to him. She told him to return to his lodge and abide in it until the Moon was again round and then go upon the World, where he would find the sons of Tate. When he found them he must with his power as a wizard aid them in the work they were doing. When this work was done, she told him to go to the lodge of Tate, and then he could forever afterwards go upon the World as he wished.

He did as he was bidden. He found the sons of Tate camped for the night, for they were making their journey. He said, "Ho, my grandchildren," and asked permission to camp with them that night. Because Yata was the firstborn, he was the leader of the party. He answered in a surly manner and turned his back towards the old man. But, Okaga, the fourth-born, spoke kindly and bade the wizard sit on his side of the campfire. When the brothers ate, the old man said he was hungry. Yata replied that he should not travel without food, for he had none to give away; but Okaga gave him some of his food which he kept in a little bag. The old man ate much of it, but when he returned the bag to Okaga it was full of food. Ever afterwards, it remained full of good food, though Okaga often ate from it until he was satisfied.

When they had eaten, the three older brothers wrapped their robes about them and lay down to sleep. Okaga gave his robe to the old man and it spread until it was so large that both Okaga and the old man could lie upon it and cover with it. So they slept together that night.

In the morning, the robe was small and light, but ever afterward it remained like new, and would stretch so that Okaga could lie upon it and cover with it at the same time. He asked the brothers where they wished to go. They told him that their father had sent them to make the four directions and put them on the edge of the World. He told them that he lived on the edge of the World, and could guide them to it, and that if they would do as he bade them, he could bring them there quickly.

They agreed to do as he would tell them. Then he gave each of them a pair of moccasins, for before this their feet had always been bare. He showed them how to put them on and bade them stand side by side with him. Then Yata said his direction should be first because it was his birthright to be first in everything and that his father had told him that his direction must be on the edge of the World where the shadows are longest at midday. He ordered the old man to guide them to that place. Then the old man told them that with the aid of the moccasins they could step from hilltop to hilltop far away. He bade Yata step first; but he was afraid and would not move. Then the old man bade Eya, the second-born, to step, and he did so and was soon on a hilltop far away. Then Yata stepped forward and was beside Eya. Yanpa, the third-born, then stepped, and he too stood beside his brothers. When the three brothers had gone, the old man asked Okaga to come with him; they stepped together and went far beyond the three brothers. He called them. When they came he told them that they could travel best under Clouds and immediately it became so Cloudy that neither the sun nor the Sky could be seen. They traveled under the Clouds more swiftly than the Birds could fly and in the evening they came to a high Mountain where the old man told them to camp that night. In the morning he told them to go over the Mountain and there they would find the edge of the World and could set up a great heap of stones. This was the first direction.

When the first direction was made, they saw the Sun. They saw that the Mountain stood where the Sun went down at the close of the day's journey. When they saw this, Yata raged, for this was Eya's direction and it was first. The old man stood before the brothers and told Yata that because he was cruel and surly, and a coward afraid to step first in the work his father had sent him to do, his birthright had been taken from him and given to Eya and that Eya would forever be considered first in all things. Then Yata hid his face and wept.

Wohpe dwelt in the tipi of old Tate and served him and his sons. The skins she dressed were soft and white; the moccasins she made were good and comfortable; the food she prepared was always abundant. She kept the fire burning and the talk pleasant so that all were happy in her presence.

Yata said to his brothers, "I want Wohpe for my woman." Yanpa replied, "You are too cold and cruel for Wohpe. Were she alone with you, she would soon perish. Remember your touch upon her dress. Wohpe should have a man who is happy and has no cares. I want her for my woman." Then Eya said, "Wohpe delights to serve others. This is her happiness. My pleasure is to be served. I would have her for my woman."

Thus they disputed, while Okaga said nothing and Yum fled to his father's tipi. They strove day by day each to still the others and make his claims good, till Okaga said, "Brothers, ask Wohpe. Whom she chooses she should serve," and they were quiet.

Yata said to Wohpe, "I want you for my woman. I am strong and my will is right. I am dreaded, for I am mighty. I will give you a part in my powers. Will you be my woman?"

Said Eya, "Wohpe, if my rest is undisturbed I do no harm. My evening's walk is my only want. Only when I am called early in the day do I fume and plague others that I may be left at my ease. Will you be my woman?"

Wohpe heard them and looked into the eyes of Okaga. That was all. Then she said, "He who will do that which pleases me most, in his robe will I stand, and him will I serve."

With this decision they must abide: the brothers were again at wordy war over who should first make an offering for the pleasure of Wohpe.

When Wohpe came to stay with Tate, he gave a feast to Taku Wakan. He consulted with his sons as to whom he should invite. They first chose the Wakan Tanka. Wi was the first chosen because he was Wakan Tanka. Hanwi, his wife, was the second chosen because she was Wakan Tanka. Inyan was the fourth because they were Wakan Tanka.

These four, with Tate, were the chiefs of Taku Wakan and formed the council. They made the rules by which all things should be governed. Then others were invited: the Unktehi who are the Wakan of the waters, the Unkheegila who are the Wakan of the lands, the Wakinyan who are the Wakan of the air; the

Tunkan who is the Wakan of the rocks, the Tatanka who is the Wakan of the Buffalo; the Can Oti who are the Wakan of the forests; the Hohngica who are the Wakans of the tipis; the Nagi because they are the Wakan of the shadows. These Tate told his sons to invite.

Okaga made the invitation wands. They were twice as long as his foot, meaning to travel with both feet; decorated with bright colors, meaning a joyous festival; and tipped with a red plume, meaning that Wakan business was to be discussed. The West Wind was to deliver them.

Old Tate gave a feast because Wakan Wohpe came to live with him. Wohpe made invitation sticks and ornamented them beautifully. Tate sent them out by his sons. They took the sticks to Iktomi, Ikcegeli, Inyan, Wasicun, Wakinyan, Takuskanskan , Tunkan, Hoya and many others.

On the day they met, both the Sun and the Moon shone. The brothers each brought his own kind of food, which Wohpe prepared. They feasted. Then they held a council in which Tate held the place of honor and told stories. Iktomi asked each for his story. Tate told of his origin. He told of the birth of his sons, of their characteristics, of the coming of the Wohpe, and of his hopes for grandchildren.

Ikchegila told of his origin and his powers. Inyan told of his origin. Wasicunpi told of their origin, their home, their pleasure, and powers. Wakinyan told of their origin, their kinds, powers, hates and likes. Taku Skan-Skan told of his origin and power. Tunkan and Hoya related their origin and powers. Iktomi tricked them and lied.

Then the guests said to Tate, "You have given presents to each of us as we desired. What can we give to you?" He said, "It is because of my daughter, Wohpe, that you have feasted. Give your presents to her." So they asked her what she would have. She sang her reply:—

"The Sun is my father. The Sun is all wise.
The Moon is my mother. The Sun is all powerful.
Let no one have power over them. No one has power over them."

They all agreed that no one would have power over the Sun and the Moon. But Iktomi played a trick on the Wankinyan and often hid the face of the Sun and the Moon, while Hoya was so greedy that he would bite away a portion of the Moon. They then asked Wohpe if she did not want something for herself. She arose and stood by Okaga, who folded his robe about her. She said, "I want a tipi for Okaga and myself. A place for him and his brothers."

They made the World and all there is in it for them. Iktomi made the unpleasant things. Old Tate came and dwelt with them, but he left his powers at the old tipi. Then they all found that it was good and came to dwell on the Earth. Iktomi stirred up strife between the brothers, so they agreed to dwell in different places, but each would visit the other.

Yata dwells in the regions of the pines. Eya dwells in the mountains where the Sun retires to rest. Yanpa dwells where the great waters are, where the Sun begins his daily journey to view the whole World. Okaga and Wohpe have their tipi in the center of the World where the Sun is highest, and little Yum lives with them. Each year they come and bring life and warmth, but as soon as they turn their backs, Yata brings cold and death. Then the birds fly to Okaga and beg him to come to their help. When they come to his tipi, they find him and Wohpe so contented and happy, that they return rejoicing, and mate and raise their young.

Tate gives presents to all the guests.

Then they all dance. Yum dances better than all and is the favorite, but Yata hates him for this. Then the Wasicun dance and Wohpe dances with them and her hair shines and flashes. Since then, when the Wasicun dance there are flashes of light (the Aurora Borealis).

Waziya joins with Yata. Waziya is the Man from the North (the region of the pines). They do many things that are strange in order to amuse the company. Iktomi gives the choice of color. They choose white. Then Yanpa does things to amuse his company. Iktomi gives him a choice of colors. He chooses blue. Then Okaga does things so wonderful that the company never tires of watching him. Iktomi gives him a choice of colors, and he chooses red. Then Wohpe asks Okaga to do some favor for each one of the guests, and he promises to do so. Okaga asked Ikcegila what he most desired, and he said he wanted to have power over everything. Okaga asked where he wanted his power. He answered that he wanted his power in his horns and his tail. So he received power. But Iktomi made his horn very soft and his tail very brittle. His women lived on the earth and his home was in the water.

Then Okaga asked Inyan what he most desired, and he said he wished to be able to resist anything. Okaga made him very hard and very large so that nothing could give him pain; but Iktomi made him very brittle so that he would break in pieces but remain undestroyed. Then the Wasicun were asked what they most desired, and they said they wished to be invisible. They were made invisible, but Iktomi deprived them of form or shape so that when they wished to communicate with others they had to steal the form of something else. Then the Wakinyan were asked what they most desired. They said they wished loud voices and bright eyes. Their wishes were granted, but Iktomi made their voices terrible and the glance of their eyes destructive.

Then Takuskanskan was asked what he most desired, and he asked to have powers over everything moving in order to protect it and do it good. He was given the power, but Iktomi made him a very sleepy one. Then Tunkan was asked what he most desired, and he said he wanted many children, so that he would be revered and cared for. They were promised him, but Iktomi promised that his children should strive among themselves, and forget him save when in trouble. Then Eya was asked what he most desired. He said he wanted to have plenty to eat at all times, so he was promised this, but Iktomi declared that he would always be hungry and his food would give him pain. Other gifts were given to the other guests.

"In those days came John the Baptist, preaching in the wilderness of Judea, And saying, Repent ye: for the kingdom of heaven is at hand." St. Matthew 3:1-2

GOOD MEDICINE
IN
GLACIER
NATIONAL
PARK

INTRODUCTION

A drive through Glacier National Park, in NorthWest Montana, today, gives many people a wonderful opportunity to see vast areas of unspoiled wilderness land from the comfort of their automobile seats. Few of these people are aware of the tremendous spiritual value that this region has held for those who have ventured out to seek it.

For untold centuries the wonders of the Glacier National Park country were held in awe by various Native tribes such as the Blackfoot, Kutenai, Stoney and Cree. The Blackfoot People were jealously guarding this region from all intruders when they were first visited in the area by white men during the early 1800's. These People, who were well acquainted with the vast NorthWest country, considered the many peaks within the park as "The Backbone of the World." A wealth of myths, tales, and stories of the Blackfoot days in the Glacier Park region were recorded by historians, both Native and white. This booklet presents a selection of these accounts. The photographs that accompany them were taken at a time when tipis were still a common sight within the park boundary, and when campfires still illuminated the wrinkled faces of the old men and women who related many of these stories as firsthand experiences.

Today, the outward signs of Native life are all gone from Glacier National Park. Gone are the tipis, and gone are the old, wrinkled faces. Yet, the Spiritual Powers that attracted the People of the Past are as strong today as they were then. Read these stories. Study these pictures. Then, visit one of the places that sounds most appealing to YOU. Walk to a secluded spot and sit down. Study closely all that surrounds you. It really hasn't changed at all! The spiritual powers that enchanted the people of the past who sought them are just as available to the people of today who will seek them.

THE TIPI CAMP

How inviting look the waters of Punak'iksi Ituktai—the Cut Bank River—on a Summer's afternoon. How refreshing looks the green field that winds along as a narrow valley next to the river. Nearby is a forest of towering pines, whose countless numbers lie like an endless Buffalo robe at the foot of the majestic, snow-covered mountains.

Along the river's bank is a small camp of half a dozen tipis. Colorful religious designs on the covers of some of the tipis tell that they belong to the Blackfoot Tribe. Divided into three divisions, the powerful Blackfoot, for years ruled the plains and Eastern mountain passes in Montana and Alberta. The mountains that bring forth the waters of Cut Bank River were well-known for their spiritual powers and were jealously guarded by the Blackfoot as their own sacred domain.

The tipi camp by the river amply illustrates the close relationship between its occupants and the surrounding Nature. Tipi doors all open to the East, out of respect to the direction of Sun's first rays each morning. Sun is representative of the Great Spirit, which includes all the Universe. It is Sun's energy which stimulates all Life.

Sun's afternoon rays help create a relaxing atmosphere among the tipis of the small camp. Near the river sit the men, gathered to tell and hear stories. A long-stemmed pipe is being passed around the circle of men, each one smoking leisurely. Whenever necessary, the pipe is refilled with tobacco from a fringed bag of

STABS-BY-MISTAKE, SUN WOMAN, AND LITTLE OTTER IN CUTBANK CANYON

softly-tanned Deerhide. The tobacco is a mixture of native plants, herbs, and bark; sweet of taste and aromatic of odor.

Not far from the men are gathered their women and children. The younger children are playing with buckskin dolls and miniature bows and arrows. Some of the older children are putting up a play-tipi, while others are watching the women's skillful hands as they make and decorate clothes for their families. Using sinew thread, made from strips of animal muscle, they are sewing together soft buckskin hides and decorating them with dyed porcupine quills and tiny glass beads that were imported from Europe.

Many of the stories being told by the men are about their own experiences on war trails or with hunting parties. Every social and religious gathering is an opportunity for those with brave deeds or adventuresome tales to stand before an enthused audience and relate them. Many stories were so popular that they were proudly told again and again. Often they were passed from generation to generation. Sometimes they gained so much romance by retelling that they were better called myths than stories. Let us hear about one that was told often when camp was made along the Cut Bank River.

THE MEDICINE BEAR OF CUT BANK RIVER

This happened not long after the time the first white men visited the Blackfoot. A small band of People was camped down by the Cut Bank River one Summer. It was early in the evening, and the men were gathered in one of the tipis to talk. Outside, children were still playing, while the women gathered firewood and brought in water. One of these women carried her pouch of water right into the tipi in which the men were gathered, thereby interrupting the conversation. While down at the river, she told the surprised men, a stranger had watched her from a clump of bushes. She had hurried back without arousing any suspicion.

Quickly, the men gathered their weapons from their tipis. Silently, they made their way down to the water's edge. On the opposite shore they saw the members of a small enemy war party preparing to cross the river towards camp. They watched silently as the would-be attackers removed their clothes, wrapped their weapons with them, and held them over their heads while crossing the river.

Only the flowing water could be heard in the night air until—suddenly—came loudly the war-cries of the watchers as they attacked the war party of startled men. Left and right the enemy fell, until only their chief got to shore alive.

Some of the warriors watched the thicket in which the chief had managed to hide, while the rest took the trophies of battle to which they were entitled. From within the thicket came a torrent of insults, accompanied by loud grunting sounds and challenges to those outside to come in and fight. Remembering the chief's ferocity in the open, no one dared to enter the dense brush to accept the challenge.

It was not until the following morning that the men were able to charge the thicket and slay their opponent. Around his neck they found a string of huge Grizzly Bear claws. Recalling the sounds he had made while fighting, the men knew that this was a Grizzly Bear Medicine Man. They feared his power, even as he lay dead. Camp was immediately packed up and moved.

The tipis had not even been set up at the new campsite when a great commotion took place. A very powerful Grizzly Bear had come into camp and knocked down one of the lodges and killed its occupants. The rest of the People tried to escape, but several more were killed before the huge Bear disappeared.

For many years after that battle camps that were made near the site were troubled by a large Grizzly Bear. The People felt that this was the enemy chief. They named the Bear Akoch'kitope—the Medicine Grizzly—and they feared his supernatural power.

Camps made along the Cut Bank River were strategically located. An ancient trail follows the river for many miles. Some parts of it can still be seen today. Other parts were widened to become automobile roads. The trail has been best preserved amid some of the tall stands of timber that border the river.

Hunters once used the Cut Bank Trail to reach the Buffalo herds which grazed on the plains to the East. Warriors used the same trail to cross the Rocky Mountains and raid the Indian tribes on the West side. These Westside Tribes, as they were called by the Blackfoot, included the Flathead, Kutenai, and Pend d' Oreille. They often hunted for Elk and Sheep on the Western slopes of the mountains of Glacier Park. They also used the Cut Bank Trail to cross the mountains for occasional Buffalo hunts on the plains. Such hunting parties often consisted of members from several Westside tribes, making up a sizeable group. Small parties constantly faced the danger of attack by the more numerous and aggressive Blackfoot. The Blackfoot considered the Westsiders thieves for "stealing" their Buffalo, and fierce battles were fought whenever the two sides met. Such a battle once took place in the thick woods near the head of the canyon that lies East of the summit of Cut Bank Pass.

BATTLE AT CUT BANK PASS

This battle was the result of a chance meeting between two war parties on the Trail. Headed downhill were the mounted members of a group led by the famous Blackfoot Chief Siyeh—the respected and fearless Mad Wolf. They were returning from successful horse raids against the Westside People. Hearing the sounds of horses coming uphill, Mad Wolf had his men take cover to see who it might be. The other group turned out to be a war party of Kutenai, heading home after a successful raid on the Blackfoot.

Mad Wolf opened the battle by shooting the Kutenai chief from his horse. Although caught by surprise, the Kutenai outnumbered their enemies and held their ground. Mad Wolf pursued the wounded Kutenai chief through the dense brush and finally killed him. As he reached down to take his enemy's scalp a familiar sight shocked him. Tied to the Kutenai chief's belt were the scalps of Mad Wolf's own two brothers. They had started out with Mad Wolf, on this war expedition, but turned back home before crossing the mountains. They had met their fate along the Cut Bank Trail, just like this Kutenai chief met his fate.

Mad Wolf told his retreating warriors of the discovery, and then led them on a violent attack for revenge that ended in death for all but one of the Kutenai, that one being an old woman. They gave her food and extra clothing and sent her on her way home, praying that someday they would be helped when in need, just as they had helped this old woman and shown mercy. Mad Wolf died of old age, in his home near the Cut Bank River, in 1903. North of Upper St. Mary's Lake is Mount Siyeh and Siyeh Pass, both named in honor of the respected chieftain.

TWO MEDICINE LODGES

From Cut Bank Pass to the South and East another trail winds its way from the rugged crags North of Mount Rising Wolf down to the lush and mystic meadows and forests of the three lakes in the Two Medicine Lodges area. The campground that is known today as Two Medicine Lake is located in a most spiritual area. Campers and trailers stand today where tipis and Medicine Lodges stood in the past. This was a favorite camping place for the Blackfoot People, and many religious ceremonies were conducted there. To the Blackfoot the place was known as Ma'toki Okas Omu'ksikimi—the Lake of the Two Medicine Lodges.

The very name—Two Medicine Lodges—recalls a time of deep spiritual need in the history of the Blackfoot Tribe. It was here, at the foot of majestic Mount Rising Wolf and the outlet of middle Two Medicine Lake, that the Blackfoot People gathered in a long-ago time of drought and famine. The Buffalo had left the neighboring plains, streams had gone dry, and only in the vicinity of these lakes could the women find enough berries to calm the hunger of their families. Because of the desperate need, and the many People who were gathered, it was decided to build two Lodges for the great Medicine Lodge Ceremony—the grand annual religious festival of the Blackfoot Tribe.

The spiritual leaders of the People who had gathered—the Medicine Men and Holy Women—fasted and prayed, asking the Spirits of the Universe for aid. Through dreams and visions these People were told to send seven of their wisest patriarchs North to Chief Mountain. Here was thought to dwell the spirit of the Winds, for these often blow fiercely along the walls of the 9,000 foot high mountain.

The old men were chosen, and soon found themselves at the foot of the noble mountain. A strong wind had been blowing across the plains, growing stronger as they approached. The summit of Chief Mountain was barely visible to the old men, as they struggled through the dust and debris that filled the air. None of the party had the strength or courage to climb the desolate reaches of the wind-swept mountainside. They went back to the camp by the Lake and told the People of their failure.

Another group of men was chosen to pray on Chief Mountain. This time the selection was made from among the daring and brave young warriors. Fourteen were chosen to go. Their arrival at the Mountain was also marked by terrific winds and almost unbearable dust. Wrapping their robes tightly about them and leaving behind their travelling packs, the group of warriors climbed up towards the forbidding peak. As they neared the summit they were almost overcome by heavy clouds that cut off all visibility to their wind-swollen eyes. Here, they sat down in a tight circle and began the prayers and songs that make one's mind leave the body in search of spiritual contact.

Rain drops fell steadily on the party of men as they climbed back down the mountain's side. Clouds covered the top of Chief Mountain like an immense turban, and reached out for the plains—North and South—like long, white wings. The much-needed rain that fell from these clouds brought back life to the Earth that it entered. Great was the rejoicing among the People, and many were the offerings of thanks that were hung in trees and on boulders as signs of appreciation to the unseen Spirits who had helped them.

SCENE OF THE PAST AT TWO MEDICINE CAMPGROUND

Many a young man had his favorite sacred place there around Two Medicine Lake, where he went to be alone with the wonders of Nature and the Spirits of the Universe. Visions were sought during sleep or in deep meditation at such lonely, spiritual places. The vision might tell the seeker of something to do, or to avoid doing. More often, the vision showed the seeker certain items, ceremonies, and songs which could be used at a later time to again summon the spiritual feeling that was present at the time of the vision. Taking only a robe for warmth, and a pipe for meditation, the vision seeker often spent several days and nights trying to establish communication and understanding with the many elements of Nature.

Besides being a most spiritual place to camp, the area of the Two Medicine Lodges was once a wonderful hunting ground. In those days game conservation in the Park region was not required. Hunters were few, and animals were so very many. What the hunters did shoot, however, they made all possible use of. The meat of a fine buck, for instance, was roasted and eaten, or dried and stored for later meals. The hide was tanned and sewn into shirts, dresses, leggings, moccasins, pouches, and quivers. Thin strips were cut from the left-over pieces of hide for use as strings and straps. The hooves were cleaned and boiled, then carved or strung plain with bead spacers on leather straps to make jingling bandoleers and necklaces. The horns made nice handles for knives and awls. With holes drilled through them they were used as arrow-shaft straighteners. The teeth were often strung on necklaces. Leg bones made good brushes for applying native powder paint to large surfaces. Properly cut, these bones make won-

◀ STABS-BY-MISTAKE ▲ CAMP IN TWO MEDICINE VALLEY

RUNNING WOLF'S SACRED LODGE ON TWO MEDICINE LAKE

derful pipes for smoking. Intestines make good paint powder pouches, as well as containers for the Porcupine quills used in decorating. Tendon fibers make the sinew for sewing and beading. Even the hair on the Deer's tail has a use in making the dance roaches which are worn in the hair. The true hunter would not consider killing an animal merely to take a small portion for glory.

Back in the days when there were tipi camps at Two Medicine the hunter had a wide choice of game animals and birds that lived in the surrounding valley and woods. Fortunately, these animals can all still be seen here. The lakes abound with fish (although some People in the old days never ate them for religious reasons), and waterfowl visitors are still frequent. Higher up the hunters used to seek the Mountain Goat and the Bighorn Sheep. The Naturalist-Writer George Bird Grinnell wrote that Rising Wolf told him: "The Gray Sheep used to be very plenty. . . .in old times when the Piegans were camped. . . .he has gone up on top (of mountains) with a lot of young fellows and driven the Sheep down to the plain below where the People were waiting on horseback. There they would kill hundreds of them. . . .their skins were used for making war shirts and women's dresses."

Grinnell loved to camp and explore the Glacier Park region. He was called Fisher Cap by his many Blackfoot friends, some of whom took him for his first visit to the Park area in 1885. He was so inspired that he used his persuasion in national articles and important friendships to make the area a national park. He would have preferred that it remain a sacred domain for the Blackfoot People, but he realized that the greed of the advancing new "civilization" would find some way to swindle the tribe out of this choice land and then destroy its primitive beauty.

TWO-GUNS-WHITE-CALF AND COMPANIONS HAVING
A DANCE IN THE EARLY PARK DAYS. TRIBAL
JUDGE BIRD RATTLER SINGS AT LEFT; JOHNNY
GROUND WATCHES BEHIND TWO GUNS.

TWO MEDICINE CAMPGROUND IN TIMES GONE BY:
READY FOR THE MEDICINE LODGE CEREMONY AT
THE FOOT OF MOUNT RISING WOLF.

The hunters are gone now, but not so the game. Look up to the higher reaches of Mount Rising Wolf from your campsite at its feet, the Two Medicine Campground. Early in the morning or late in the afternoon you may catch the movement of tiny white specks. With field glasses you can watch the Goat or Sheep as they wind their way along treacherous trails in a world that belongs almost exclusively to them. It required great skill and patience for a hunter to come within shooting distance of these wary animals. It required just as much in strength and daring for the hunter to carry the carcass of his kill back down the precipitous trails.

RISING WOLF

And who was the Rising Wolf whom this noble mountain is named for? He was the trader and trapper Hugh Monroe who, at the age of seventeen, was the first white man known to have visited this part of the Rockies. He was an employee of the great Hudson's Bay Company and roamed the Blackfoot country as an adopted member of that tribe. He married a young Blackfoot woman, joined Blackfoot hunting and war parties, and was given the name Makwi

Powaksin—Rising Wolf. He loved to camp and hunt in the area around the mountain that bears his name. When he died, in 1896, he was buried along the Two Medicine River, not far from the mountain.

When not in need of the fine pelts of the Goat or Sheep up on the high ridges, the native hunters preferred to seek game in the valleys and forests down by the lakes. Deer, Elk, and Moose have always been plentiful in the area. Bears, too, are quite common in the region. Many a hunter was foiled in his tracking by suddenly meeting a Grizzly Bear in his path. The Blackfoot name for the Grizzly is "the Real-Bear," and the People most always gave the animal wide berth. Few warriors cared to prove their bravery the way one well-remembered Blackfoot hunter did. Weasel Tail was armed only with his good hunting knife when he engaged a huge Grizzly in a hand-to-hand encounter. The Battle was short, brave Weasel Tail emerging as the victor. Forever after he proudly wore the Grizzly's big claws on a necklace.

On the road to Two Medicine Camp, not far below the main lake, is a most spectacular waterfall. A short and interesting trail leads the visitor from the paved road back to an enchanting trout pool, at the head of which is the waterfall. It is known today as Trick Falls. It was a favorite bathing place of the legendary Pitamakan, after whom the Blackfoot named it. Pitamakan was a warrior's name which means Running Eagle, but it was earned, in this case, by a brave Blackfoot woman.

THE STORY OF PITAMAKAN

Pitamakan was a young girl known as Weasel Woman when both of her parents were killed. With her brothers and sisters she worked hard to keep their orphaned family together in one tipi. By necessity she learned to do many of the chores usually done by men. So it was that she joined one day a war party bound for the Westside tribes. She did so without telling anyone, and against the wishes of some of the men in the party. The party was successful, and the young girl returned with several fine horses which she had captured. The People were amazed by her bravery, and an old Medicine Man gave her the name of an honored Blackfoot chief of the past—Pitamakan.

There followed, for Pitamakan, a career of horse raiding. She even led some of her own war parties against enemy tribes, for no man was ashamed to join with her. Whenever leaving for a raid Pitamakan would exchange her woman dress for warrior's clothing. Her takings of horses were many, and she counted coup on three men whom she herself killed. Her end came when she was discovered one night leading horses from the midst of an enemy camp. Her Blackfoot People kept alive the memories of her with stories about her exploits, and by naming these falls for her.

THE OLD WAY OF TRAVELLING THROUGH THE PARK. OLD THREE BEARS, THERE, WAS A GREAT ORATOR AMONG THE BLACKFOOT PEOPLE.

ST. MARY'S LAKES

The area around the St. Mary's Lakes was popular in the old days because of the large camping space in the valley by the lower lake, and the abundance of game that was found there. Rising Wolf took one of the early Jesuit missionaries (Father DeSmet) to the lakes in 1846. There he helped plant a wooden cross at the foot of the lower lake, while the priest said a prayer and christened the lake St. Mary. The Blackfoot People know Saint Mary by the name Patoaki—the Good-Spirit-Woman. The lakes, however, were known to them by the name Puhtomuksi Kimiks—the Lakes-Inside.

Rising Wolf first visited these lakes in 1816, when his adopted Blackfoot People camped down by the lower one of the two. That same location later became his favorite hunting and trapping place. With his Blackfoot wife and four children he spent many seasons there, collecting furs and enjoying the freedom of nature. Sometimes he was forced to fight off war parties from enemy tribes like the Crows, Assiniboin, and Yankton Sioux. His lodge was always protected by a stockade, or a trench dug around its perimeter. He kept every member of the family armed and trained to help in defense. His take of furs included Beaver and Otter. For hides and meat of larger game he could take Moose along the lake, Deer and Elk in the valley, or Sheep and Goats high in the mountains. Even Buffalo herds came to this, the Western boundary of their home on the great plains.

STABS-BY-MISTAKE WITH HIS SACRED MEDICINE, AT THE LOWER END OF UPPER ST. MARY'S LAKE. SURROUNDED BY MOUNTAINS ARE THESE "LAKES-INSIDE." LIKE NATURE'S BOWL OF TREASURES IS THIS COUNTRY: LAKES AND STREAMS FULL OF FISH, VALLEYS AND WOODS FULL OF GAME, TREES AND SKIES FULL OF BIRDS.

In the long ago members of the Crow tribe made their home in parts of Glacier Park. A popular story around Blackfoot campfires tells how the Crow were driven from the Glacier area down to their present homeland in SouthEast Montana by the Blackfoot. At that time most of the Blackfoot bands were living North of the United States border, in Alberta and Saskatchewan. A Blackfoot man named One Horn came down to the St. Mary's Lakes area to camp with the Crows and discuss with them his desires for a permanent peace between the two tribes.

ONE HORN'S PEACE MISSION

One Horn stayed with the Crows for some time in their camp by the St. Mary's Lakes. His women kept up their household there, amid the Crow tipis. They had many guests and, in turn, were often invited to the lodges of others. The Crow chief and One Horn became good friends, and often went hunting together.

So it was until a Crow braggard, one night, told his fantastic story of bravery against the Blackfoot. The tipi was filled with guests that night. The Crow claimed that he had been wounded and his partner killed, while they were attacked by a whole village of the Blackfoot. Despite a bad arrow wound, the Crow stated, he made an heroic escape through all the People. To prove his tale, he produced the Blackfoot arrow and showed everyone there his wound.

One Horn laughed when he saw the arrow. "That arrow is my own," he told the listeners. "I surprised two horse thieves in our camp one morning, and killed one. The other one dropped his weapons and ran. I wounded him with an arrow from my quiver." At that he reached into his quiver and pulled out an identical arrow and laid it before the murmuring crowd. The braggard hurriedly left the lodge, while the guests jeered him.

One night, soon after, one of the Crow chief's wives stole into One Horn's lodge and brought him a warning. She had overheard her man agree to help the braggard kill One Horn for the price of five horses. The next morning One Horn dressed in his finest clothes, took his weapons, and rode his horse into the middle of the camp circle. From there he shouted to the Crow chief, for all to hear:

"My friend, your plan to help that braggard in killing me has been found out I have the spiritual guidance of my Grizzly Bear Medicine, and I challenge you both to fight me here, now." The Crow chief made no reply, and remained in his tipi. The braggard, whose lodge was at the other end of the camp, grabbed his horse and hurriedly rode into the woods.

One Horn packed up his belongings and returned North to his People. After telling them of his adventures he called on the men to help him in driving the Crow people far away from the Blackfoot country. War parties were formed among all three Blackfoot divisions, and the Crows were soon put to flight. They never again moved back to the Glacier Park country.

LAKE OF THE JEALOUS WOMEN

Nestled amid towering mountain peaks, melting glaciers, dark canyons, and green, wooded valleys is the awe-inspiring Lake McDermott. The Lake's blue waters are Nature's mirrors. They are able to describe the surrounding scenery like no man's words. To the Native People of long ago, such a scene was an experience that no modern form of entertainment could rival.

Lake McDermott was sometimes known as Beaver Woman's Lake, but is best remembered in old stories as Jealous Women's Lake. It was given this name by the Kutenai People, from the Westside, who told this story of its origin:

There once lived a young Kutenai warrior named Big Knife whose two wives were twin sisters. The family got along well, except that one sister worked quicker than the other. This sister, whose name was Weasel, also talked a lot. She sometimes complained that the other sister, whose name was Beaver, was not doing her share of work and was often trying to become Big Knife's favorite. Beaver thought Weasel to be foolish for having such bad thoughts.

Big Knife was out riding his horse one day when he came upon two Otters at the bank of the Kamoak-skasee Naya-tahtah—the Swift Current River. "What nice presents those two Otter skins would make for my women," said Big Knife to himself. He quickly strung his bow, fitted an arrow, and shot one of the Otters. Before he could shoot again, however, the other Otter disappeared. He took the one skin home and gave it to Beaver, telling them both that he would go back the next day to get the other skin for Weasel.

Big Knife searched all the next day for the other Otter, but could not find it. For several days he searched in other areas near camp, but nowhere did he see another Otter.

Weasel, meanwhile, was getting more cross at home. She told Beaver that the Otter skin was sure proof of her favored position with their man. Beaver could not convince Weasel that their man was very distressed about not finding another Otter.

Finally, one day, Weasel told her twin sister that the two could no longer live together in the same lodge. "I will challenge you in any way to determine which of us shall remain in this lodge with Big Knife," she told her sister.

The two then decided that they would swim the lake by which they were camped, up and back until only one was left swimming.

So it came that Beaver found herself crawling up on the lake's shore. She looked all around the quiet lake top, but could not detect any sign of her sister. She went home weeping, and Big Knife wept too, when he heard what had taken place. Together they wept, and for a long time they were sad. It is so easy to disturb the beauty of Nature.

SOME PLEASANT THOUGHTS

LIFTING HIS STONE-BOWLED PIPE, OLD MAN TAIL-FEATHERS-COMING-OVER-THE-HILL MUTTERS A PRAYER FOR US:

Hi-Yo Spirits With Us. . . . Guide Us As We Follow
The Many Paths That Lead Us Through Life. . . Show
Us In Dreams The Ways To Live Right. . . . Give Us
The Strength To Learn From Our Failures. . . . SUN
Give Us Warmth With Your Eternal Light.

WITH TEARS PLEADS OUR MOTHER EARTH:

Remain Close To Me, My Children.
Pray To Your Father—Sun
Live In Harmony With Nature
Respect The Will Of EVERY One!

As The Winds That Blow, Here, Let My Mind Wander. . . .
As The Tree That Stands Here, Give Me Strength And Old Age.
Let Me Bend, And Mold, To Stronger Forces. . . . Let Solid
Ground, Forever, Hold My Feet.

I Am Three Bears—An Old Pikuni—Here In The Mountains. . .
I Came To Think—To Look Ahead—To Hope And Pray:

. . . .May My Ancestors—In All The World—Still Have The
Wisdom, To Live With Nature. . . . To Come and Pray, To
ALL, Our Spirits There. . . .

And So Was Crossed The "Backbone Of The Earth" In The Days When Time Was Counted By Moons And Snows. . . . Two-Guns-White-Calf And Friends Leaving Two Medicine.

Horses! Fleet On Foot—Flowing In Mane—Gentle In Character—And Ever Aware.

Together: Man And Horse. The Strength To Travel . . . .The Ability To Know. Trusting Each Other To Trust In Nature. . . . Trusting All Others To Trust The Same.

Along The Rivers. . . . Throught The Forests. . . Up The Canyons. . . Into Mountains On Paths Lined With The World. . . . Every Path An Experience To Learn From: Up And Down, Left And Right, And (Like Life) Forever Luring On.

THE SPIRIT AT
HIDDEN VALLEY

A GOOD MEDICINE STORY

Illustrated by — F. N. WILSON

.... I am trying to open my eyes. I am wondering: Am I really waking up, or is this my Dream, continuing—I seemed so safe on that trail up the mountain, so safe and sure that I would reach the top. Then I fell! I fell and fell and thought so much that it was The End. Was it The End? Or was it The Beginning? How can there be The End? Does not The End mean at once a New Beginning? ....

.... But here I am, so it is no end. Here I am, hearing voices and seeing colors. A bright light I see most, and I feel as though the voices and colors are coming at me through a huge funnel—a funnel that sits upside down and fully covers me.

.... A hospital room. . . .I must be in a hospital room! Ohh—how badly did I get hurt. . . .I wonder? Waking from an operation. . . .that's it—the anesthetic must be wearing off after the operation. But I don't feel hurt. . . .drowsy, but not hurt. And this hospital room? Nurse. . . .Nurse. . . .there's a fire here! ....

The room is round—round and tall and pointed at the top. It has a framework of poles and I can see the Sky through an opening at the top. And there is smoke going up, up and out through the opening at the top. There is a fragrance to the smoke—a sweet and pungent fragrance—a distinct fragrance, though I notice there are others in the air: of foods and strange things. . . .I close my eyes. . . .

Another look: still the same. And the presence of People. I turn my head and look beside me: a strange scene of things I am not familiar with—things that look bright and colorful and alive. And there are People—amidst all the unusual things. And these People look different, somehow, than the People I am accustomed to. They are good to look at—so good to look at that I get a funny feeling by looking at them. Though they must be total Strangers, I feel that I know them—can trust them—can love them—should be here among them. . . .for whatever the reason. I Am Here: is the proof of this! I close my eyes. . . .

I look again, though the good feeling remains even with my eyes closed. A sound like sails flapping in a breeze draws my attention overhead, the sound slides downwards, making the walls of our dwelling ripple against the tall poles, and it brings with it a faint gust of cool, fresh air, followed by the sound of rustling leaves on unseen trees and bushes whose presence I suddenly feel all around. Some Birds voice their approval, and I close my eyes. . . .

For the fourth time I open my eyes, and the scene, as from a Dream, is still there. . . .I am still Here. And who are these People who are here with me? I lift myself up on an elbow—raise myself up with my hand. No one pays any attention to me—perhaps it is still a Dream. I look around:

Across from me there are some women, sewing—four women, there are. One of them is much older than the others—while two of them are about my age. One must be the Mother. Her body rocks gently with each stitch she takes with her sewing—her thoughts seem to flow with the stitches, too. . . .she looks as though pictures are there, where each stitch goes. Many small wrinkles radiate outward from the outside corner of each eye. . . .and her small, dark eyes seem to twinkle. Her hair is darkish, not too heavy, and she wears it in two braids. She is covered by a Buckskin dress which hangs almost to her ankles and is decorated from the waist up by beautiful patterns of attached beads.

The Old Lady just watches, sometimes she closes her eyes. The girls, too, are sewing something—their hands barely moving and their thoughts buried deep within their work. They are dressed in light-colored, cloth dresses, with large sleeves that hang down in loose folds. Their faces are partly hidden by their long hair, which falls down way past their shoulders. They are seated on some furs—like those beneath me. All around this neat dwelling are spread other furs. Some fine, old trunks are standing here and there. I am here, in this home—I am here, in this tipi—I am here, but I don't know where.

While I wonder whether or not to interrupt the pleasant silence which surrounds me sounds from outside draw my attention towards the door. Quiet laughing, like children playing somewhere, the bark of Dogs, the sound of water, running along. Then sounds of footsteps falling softly on the ground. A shadow approaches outside now—the doorway opens to let in light—and someone's leg. A man enters—smoothly and gently—gives me a glance and a smile comes to his face. The man has on a shirt and pants of Buckskin, long, braided hair with strips of cloth tied on the ends. He walks over—saying nothing, but still smiling—and sits beside me on the furs that are lying there. For a moment he looks into my eyes—a feeling of happiness is conveyed. Then he looks towards the door and holds his right hand out, as though inviting someone else to come inside.

Through that door you were brought into this household, he says, pronouncing clearly every letter in each word. *Why You were sent here you will find out in time. But this much I will tell you at this moment: We are your family for as long as you stay here—that is your bed, this is your lodge, ours is your food. What You were Seeking in Your life's dreaming is yours to live now— your dreams were strong, for THEY guided You here. After you've been here for a while you'll know this better—perhaps the Power of your dreams will then be clear.*

He ceases talking and sits silent for some moments, then he turns and reaches for something behind. I hadn't noticed the rear of this tipi—there are bags and pouches hanging up. Underneath the wooden tripod from which they are hanging is a mound of clean dirt, piled like an Anthill. In the center is a circle of bright orange, made from some kind of powder sprinkled there. From that circle are many lines of red going outwards—like the spokes of a wheel—all done with care. At the base of the mound lies a small pipe with a black bowl and a short, wooden stem. This is what he is reaching back for. He takes it and brings it to him from back there. He reaches back again for a small sack, which he opens, filling from it the bowl of the small pipe. He takes a stick—holds it briefly in the fire—while he raises the small pipe into the Air.

For my new son—let our first smoke bind our Spirits. Hear me, Powers who are around us Everywhere. Give my new son strength and guidance—make him happy. Let his dreams become as one with our prayers.

He looks into my eyes once again, smiling, and causes a smile to cover my face, as well. He takes the stick from the fire and holds it in the pipe bowl, puffing, at the same time, on the other end. The gray smoke curls upward—the fine smell goes all around us. He blows a whisp of the smoke up, four whisps to the directions, and another whisp to the ground. He turns the pipe in a Sun-wise direction and hands it to me, stem first, without a sound. I do likewise, as I just saw him do in his smoking, but he corrects me as I hand the pipe back to him.

When passing a pipe to another, he says to me, in a kindly way, *you must turn the pipe in the direction Sun travels, and thus wish your brother a good day.*

After we finish smoking the pipe my new Father asks me to empty the ashes from its bowl into the fireplace. As I turn to do this the Old Lady looks over at me with a smile and a wink, and says:

You'd better be careful, Sonny, that boy of mine, there, is a pretty mean father and will soon have you doing all his work so that he can stay around this lodge to bother us ladies!

My new Father smiles embarrassingly and nods his head towards the Old Lady, saying:

This is my mother. She likes to tease everyone a lot. Luckily, she is not as mean as she looks. You'll be calling her Grandma in no time, like we all do. I guess I should tell you, too, about the others in your new family, he goes on.

You may already have guessed that the older of the others, here, is your new Mother—you just call her Mom. The other two will be your sisters from now on. Then, while they continue their work and act as though they are not aware that our attention is on them, Father adds:

You may call either of them sister, or you may prefer to call them by their names. 'Long Way' is what we call her with the lighter hair, while her sister with the braided hair we call 'Good Faith'. You may even find that their names take on meaning, as you watch them in daily life. But, no matter how we may differ in some of our ways, we always seem to end each experience with that Powerful feeling of One-ness that has helped to bring You here.

After some moments of silence Father begins to rise, saying:

I think we should go outside now—the men from the camp are gathered down by the lakeshore and are expecting our company.

So I follow him out of the tipi—stepping into the Outside for my first time. Outside: standing in the warm, fresh air—a sight takes away all my senses—a sight that is more fantastic than any I have ever dreamed of—a simple and fantastic sight. Like a massive painting from a child's fairy tale book lies the scene that is before my eyes. Green and blue dominates the scene—green meadow and green forests, with a vast blue Sky above. The rocks and snow on the massive mountains, which rise up all around us, reflect the green from below and the blue from above—reflect them and combine them to take on a tone of their own which blends harmoniously that which is Above and that which is Below.

It is difficult to attempt even a walk into a painting which is so beautiful as this one—a scene so majestic—but it is almost impossible to believe that I am actually A PART of that scene! Yet, Father and I, ARE a part of it, just like the tree to our left, the tipi behind us, the Horses straight ahead, and the countless other living Spirits who surround us to add color and strength to this fantastic experience of Universal Life.

It is a short walk down the shore of the lake. Grasses and flowers grow almost to the water line, which is barely moving—like the slow breathing of a silent giant. The water is clear—of course—and for some distance out, away from shore I can see the yellow sand that rests below it, broken here and there by some stones or small growths of green plants. A stone's throw ahead of us is the gathering of men—most of them seated. Several of the younger men are off to one side, playing a lively game amongst themselves. One of them is rolling a rustic sort of wheel—about the size of a man's head—towards the others, who wait for it with arrows in their hands. As the wheel passes by, each one throws his arrow at it. A shout goes up from the participants and some of the spectators as the wheel topples over and comes to rest on the ground, one of the arrows stuck in its center. The wheel itself is made from twisted grasses which are then wrapped with a wet strip of rawhide which hardens when it dries. The wheel has numerous spokes of rawhide lacing in which the successful thrower's arrow becomes entangled. Father tells me all this, adding that the game sometimes goes on all day—often to the tune of such wagered items as tobacco and craft work.

We sit down on the ground and join the gathering, which has no air of formality about it whatever. Since Father's first mention of this, back in the tipi, I have been dreading the thought of formal introductions in front of a scrutinizing collection of wise men and minds. At the moment I do not feel that type of a situation at hand.

Father has begun a conversation with a man seated near him, who appears to be about his same age. The man has two dark braids, as do most of the men, and he is shirtless—only a necklace of not-too-large Bear claws covers his chest. He wears loose trousers of some sort of beige-colored cloth, and Buckskin moccasins. Though each man in the group looks distinct from the others, this man's description could be called typical—if I could call anything here, at this place, typical.

The young men on the side are still playing their wheel game. Some of the men gathered here are quietly conversing with each other, while others of them are sitting quietly and gazing in various far-off directions. Their features vary widely, as do the tones of their bodies. They do not appear to be related much amongst each other, physically. Yet, there is a definite air of close relations there, among everyone. It makes me wonder if I, too, may be related, somehow, to them all.

As I contemplate these various thoughts and try to absorb the Power which I know is around me my eyes notice an Old Man sitting alone, quite nearby. Somehow I have missed seeing him until now—but, suddenly, I cannot stop looking at him—something about him is like a whirlpool pulling towards it the current of my Mind. An old, wrinkled, gray-haired man with a worn shirt of leather covering the top of his body. From beneath his massive brow peer small, dark eyes at the cliffs along the opposite shore. A fur robe covers the lower half of his body—his arms resting on it, a pipe in one hand. As I look—in total rapture— he begins, softly, chanting. One by one the others stop talking to hear. The young players sit down, their game finally ended. All attention is given to the chanting of the Old One—though still scattered about at the edge of this lakeshore—All of Us who are here seem suddenly more near.

After chanting for some time, praying words with his singing, the Old One stands up and smiles kindly towards me. He says, with the tone of a kind old Grandfather:

I am glad We are All happy with this life we have here. Tomorrow I will tell our new Brother about Us, for I know he has Good Thoughts, and that his Mind will hear me clear.

. . . . Tomorrow:

. . . . So, I wait. . . . .and, finally, he comes. He wears only moccasins, with high tops covering his ankles, and a large yellow-and-brown fur, wrapped around his waist so that the legs and tail dangle down at his sides and back. He comes. . . . and he motions for me to follow. I do—I follow and say nothing.

Soon we are away from the camp circle—away from the sounds and sensations that hover there—and out into the domain of the sounds of Wind—the vast stillness that isn't—the rustling of leaves in the tree tops—Birds gliding from one to the other in the breezes up there. I follow his footsteps along a narrow path that takes us through thick bushes, where our view is limited to a few steps ahead. Now the bushes give way to a small clearing, and the path leads us through the middle of knee-deep grasses and purple flowers—Songbird halts momentarily, thrusts both arms deep into the growth, then brings his fists up to touch his left breast, at the same time he has his eyes closed, his lips are moving in silent conversation—silent prayer—then a gentle smile engulfs his face and he glances at me—glances through me, into the unseen Spirit world that is around us. All this has taken but a few moments, and already we are on our way again, following the path back into the dense bush growth and past tall tree trunks. He says nothing, and I dare not ask.

We come to a brook, half hidden by the flowers and grasses that grow along its banks and hang out over its waters—many trailing their tops in the brook's gentle current. The path turns right, here, and ascends by short, steep layers. The green growth is very low for several steps to each side of the brook, and the path is visible some ways ahead at all times. Where the path and the trees come close together the ground is covered by a carpet of brown pine needles, and a sweet and pungent odour fills the air. I pick up a handful of the needles—the odour is definitely from them—and I'm tempted to take a bite of them—they attract me so much.

Up, behind the trees of this forest, rises the massive stone face of Stone Face Mountain—a steep incline broken only by barely-visible narrow trails which run like wrinkles across the Stone Face, and a few shrub-covered knolls that stick out like small hair-covered moles from the looming Face. Father has already pointed this out to me from our camp.

Up Stone Face Mountain we climb, after leaving behind us the growth of the forest. A well-worn trail—a steep, rocky path—takes us rapidly higher, and our breath grows noticeably shorter. Up....up....up....up....the Old One keeps right on climbing and leading us like tiny explorers across the great Stone Face.

I think my body is about to give up its efforts, as the Old One finally motions towards a small knoll just up ahead—he is planning for us to halt there. We come up from below the out-cropping—it looks like a vestibule in an opera house from down here (only much larger), but, as we go around and above it, the impact of its size shrinks away with the view down the mountain, until we are standing directly above and behind it, and it suddenly seems like a small place to stand upon in the vastness of the Universe, here, up high.

From our place behind the knoll the worn trail divides into several branches—one of them leading out to the point of the out-cropping itself. From up here, now, I can see that the shrub which I saw growing from down below is actually a tiny forest of stunted and twisted pines, some of which stand twice as high as I. Everywhere I look there are droppings and track marks—the knoll must be a favorite look-out and gathering place for many of the animals hereabouts. Here and there are flat places in the grass growth—indicating some visitors have, recently made here their beds.

On the ground, before a large boulder, the Old One sits down on his fur robe—he sits so that his back leans against the boulder and his eyes can take in the breathtaking scene all around. Likewise, I sit down by him—for some time not a word can be said. Down below are the camps of the People—in the valley, by the lake, they look so small. The lake—I can see from one end to the other—like a long sheet of blue glass spread out below. The forest—like the hair upon a fur robe—a solid mass, with some additional patches growing here and there. In the distance, all around, a wall of mountains. Up above, the solid Sky—the endless Air.

His voice sounds strangely near after my eyes and Mind have wandered so far. *I come often up to this place—to see our Valley,* he says, while gazing away, out there. How many places, that he sees now, does he know close-up? How many adventures can he see in this one view?

For most of my 92 years of Life I have known this place, he now continues, *hardly anything seen from up here has changed at all. The Great Spirit of the Universe wants us to know THAT—for, compared to the Universal Power, the lives of men, like ourselves, are very small.*

It was meant that this Valley be populated by a People whose lives remain at Nature's call. For this valley enjoys complete isolation, from the wounds that other People in the World befall.

Now, since your strange arrival, you have wondered about this Valley, and how it is that all these People are living here. My name is Songbird, as was my father's before me; as tribe historian—I tell the story for one and all.

Now he has raised his left hand to his forehead, shading his eyes from the bright rays of Sun. The hand is wrinkled and scarred from old age, and only a stump remains where his small finger once was. He squints his dark eyes with a grimace that draws attention to his full lips and the remainder of his teeth—some on top, some on bottom, that are stained yellowish-brown and worn flat. Gray braids hang down behind his ears. He remains absorbed in the view he is watching—some time passes before he says anything at all. Finally, he breaks the vast silence that isn't—and again, his closeness strikes me so strongly—just two human bodies among the All.

Over there, as he points Westward, *are what we call our Sunset Wall of mountains. There, at one time was the Hidden Valley Pass. A narrow, rocky trail led from this Valley to the outside—through canyon and gorge, and sometimes along treacherous rock faces, where a misstep meant a thousand-foot fall. Through that Pass came both trappers and hunters—some to camp here and some to live here. Strong was the Valley's Spirit, through its call. Later on came some new men from far-away lands. They came to meet, to trade, explore, and just to see—what the land of our Old People had to offer—what the call of Hidden Valley could be.* He breathes deeply, several times. His hand drops from his forehead, his gaze turns to the ground. His eyes close—he is apparently reminiscing:

So it was, when I was a young boy. The new men came to Hidden Valley, and many stayed. They built a mine, a trading post, and little houses. They brought supplies, they brought their women, they brought great changes, to the silence that Hidden Valley once had.

Now, these new men got along fairly well with the Old People. They prayed (though not like we), and sang strange songs. They worked hard daily—they traded things to the Old People for meat and hides. Peace existed, by that time, among the tribes who knew this country, so little groups moved to the Valley now and then. They'd often visit, and entertain, and pray together, and the new men, when they had time, would join right in. He hums a short tune—smiles, as he explains that the new men taught some of the Old People their strange songs. All together they would sing—some old, some new songs, all loudly singing, moving bodies, feeling strong.

Came a time, late one Spring—it was almost Summer—came an old man, to this place, from somewhere West. Said a dream had brought him up—that night he'd tell us, let us decide to do whatever we feel is best. The old man was almost naked—just breechclout and blanket—but painted black from head to foot, except for a large white circle over his left breast.

That afternoon, in the camps, there was much talking, as each one wondered what the old man had to say. My father's brothers were seated and smoking—they came to talk of the old man, and to pray.

Our camp, that time, numbered twenty-four lodges—mixed bands of Blackfoot, Bloods, and Piegans, from the Plains. Camped near us were a half dozen families of Sarsi's, and next to them were some Stony's from Kutenai Plains. At the trading post were a dozen employees—their wives and families were also living there. In its courtyard were camped trappers and miners—perhaps two hundred People were gathered there.

My father and some friends set up a large lodge—one with two covers fastened together to make an oblong. Thus they made room for most of the adults who wished to hear the old man speak. Much food was cooked, and all

were served, *who felt like eating; then pipes were filled and all sat down in proper order—just whispered words while all were smoking and saying prayers.
Came in the old man—his blanket draped over his shoulders and tied in front
with two sewed-on thongs. His weight was supported by a large stick—some
Eagle feathers and some other small bird skins tied to its top. His face was still
black-smeared from painting. Down to his shoulders hung the loose locks of his
gray hair. On his cheek a large scar made a shadow, and his right eyelid was
closed—no eye was there. He walked slowly to the front of the gathering—and
though all were silent and waiting, for some time he just stood there and stared.*

'*My children,*' he began, in a strong voice for an old man,' *my Medicine has
guided me to you here. I must tell you of an event about to happen—an event
which for some of you will bring fear. For many years have my Dreams foretold
me, that the mountains would be the place of my end—ever after should continue my Spirit, among a People who will live where my thoughts shall dwell.*'
For a moment the old man paused—his face seemed to twitch and quiver—then
he cried—an old man crying—it was moving, it made everyone feel strong. He
sang a song—and from the mourning sounds in it, we all knew that it was his
death song. Right there he was singing THAT song that once his Spirits taught
him—told him to keep alone, to carry along. We all knew what would be caused
by its singing—we knew his Life here on Earth would soon be gone.

'*My children,*' he addressed us all again. '*My children, it is near here that I
must leave my body—and it is RIGHT here, where some of you will always belong. My dream has told me that the need for the Pass into this Valley is about
to pass—there is to be NO way in here, before too long. Already, my Spirits told
me, too many are coming—but soon: no more, no matter how brave or strong.
I am to go through the Pass, said my vision, go through singing my sacred death
song. Somewhere up there the mountains are to answer—the boulders falling will
take my body along. In four more days, I tell you, all of these things will
happen—just four more days, and those who stay will become strong. Ask yourselves, now, my children, if it's for you—this life that will follow, here, in this
valley; if it's for you—to live a Life that can't go wrong. For, with my Power, I
will give All my guidance to those who stay here—I'll be with you, whenever You
sing my song.*' And, again, the old man sang his song.

So, look now, again, over to Sunset Wall mountains, says Songbird slowly,
stretching his long arm towards the West. With his thumb in advance he points

carefully. *What the old man said came to pass—for gone, from over there, is the old Pass. Only four more days he lived, after that night, and then he left us, never to return.*

Songbird continues his story, after a brief pause:

There was much confusion in the camps and at the trading post, after the gathering broke up and everyone returned to their homes. There were those who thought the old man was crazy—there were those who believed him and begged him to call it off. "It is not our place to guide the destiny of the Universe—we are but humans—good for companions—but just so strong," **he** *would answer each one.*

By the second day some camps were packing—were leaving. Many new men took their packs and went along. By the fourth day the trading post was half deserted, many lodges from the Old People's camps were gone. Only lodge poles and blackened fire-pits bore solemn witness of the families no longer there— forever gone. Of those who stayed, most were sure that's what they wanted—that the old man's dream was very strong. In his final hours we gathered to hear his words of wisdom, his songs and his prayers, to keep US strong.

' Everywhere are coming new people,' he told us. ' Many of these are good people. Many of ours are good People. But the few remaining ones on both sides will cause much trouble—they will see things with only their eyes—not with their Spirits. They will forsake the Old Spirits and let the desires of daily lives design their gods. For many years will these people live that way, before their children will seek, once again, the Spirit of our life. You, who remain here, will keep alive all that Spirit so that, someday, it may grow again in the hearts and minds of a People who will be loving our Mother—Earth—with prayers and songs.'

The next morning the old man went: down, past the lakeshore, out of the valley past the waterfall, above the treeline up to the canyons and far out of sight, he went, while the People remained in camp—waiting silently. Still was the air—very quiet—till, from afar, came a rumbling sound. Everyone's eyes went up the mountains, where a dust cloud formed quickly and hid the view. Many voices joined together in prayer, while the rumbling on the mountains continued. We knew for sure, then, our fate was sealed—all together. The dream of the old man, indeed, had been strong. When the dust cleared only physical was our reaction—for all those present knew it would happen all along. The familiar sight of our old Pass was gone—so was the South side of yonder mountain. For several days, words were seldom spoken, but the bonds of brotherhood quickly grew strong.

Few of us are left today from the original People in this Valley, but the same Spirit exists today as did back then. For all these years we knew someday our Dreams would be answered—someday a new old-time-spirit People would come along.

That is why You are here with Us, now! You were guided here by the Spirits of the Universe because You looked to those Spirits of the Universe for guidance—because You believe they exist and have met them in Your Dreams and visions. All together We can make great things happen with All the Spirits who are here for Us to find.

Physically, we here in this Valley have been very fortunate. Many things to help us were stored for trapping, trading post, and for the mine. We have been careful to use just what we really needed, and to use each thing as long as it continues to have some use left. How many knives we've made anew, when they were broken; how many handles, for all our axes, were made with knives. How many clothes were worn to shreds, then sewed together, to make a new thing with a new purpose, in our simple lives. With pencils we all learned the art of writing, with needles every man and woman sews. With nails and saws we build Winter-time housing; with pots and pans we cook all our Natural foods.

But, most of all, is the strength of our isolation—it's brought together all our People to one belief: that we're all here on this Earth for a purpose, to harm no one—to give to All—to have Belief. We believe that following Dreams is what makes one happy—when one shares happiness with others, they become happy, too. Thus, all the time, someone is happy; thus, all the time, we're happy too. . . .

. . . . Nighttime—back in the lodge of my family:

My son, did Songbird tell you, today, the story of our People here, asks Father.

Yes, I reply, *a most moving story it is—a most Powerful story. It strengthens my belief in the Power of my Dreams, which have brought me here.*

You must have had a very strong belief in your dreams to begin with, continues Father, *to have gotten here at all. We knew all along that someday someone like you would come. For You will now help us to go on to the next stage of our lives here. Nothing can go on forever without change—not even the Spirit at Hidden Valley!*

I nod my head silently—Songbird, too, made some mention of expected changes here, in the Valley, due to my presence. I wish that were not so, for I would like to spend the rest of my life here, living just as I see these good People living.

Do not worry yourself, my son, says Father when he notices my silent stare, *the goodness of this Valley will continue to be, and its Spirit will be yours as long as you wish it. But there are others in this World who should know about the Spirit—for there is enough to share with All the People of this Earth.*

I would rather not even think about the rest of the World, at this time. I can not imagine what might happen if that World found out about Hidden Valley—for some it would bring great happiness, for others only envy. But the many who control the destinies of Nature—those spiritually-insignificant but physically strong and demanding ones—I fear for the plans and schemes they would develop that would quickly destroy the Spirit at Hidden Valley.

We are not expecting to re-open a pass in order to intercourse freely with the World outside, **explains Father to my concerned look.** *We would wish for some additional People to come here with us—to bring us their skills and knowledge of positive things in exchange for the life we can give them. We would wish for more families to add new blood to our children of the future—to keep us from becoming lame without the introduction of new thoughts and new ideas. You must wait for the Summer's End Ceremony to hear more about this,* **Father concludes.** *We will seek advice, then, from our long-ago Old Ones as to what we should do, now that you have come, as they predicted.*

THE YOUNG BOY AND THE OLD LADY

I go today to pay a call on the Old Lady who lives with a young boy in a small, bark-covered lodge down by the lakeshore—there, just past the edge of the forest. I met the old lady the other day, when I came up behind her on the forest trail, where she was struggling with a large load of dried wood for her fire. I offered to carry the wood, and she shyly accepted, covering her mouth with her right hand—in modesty—as she spoke to me. She led the way to her lodge in such a fashion that no one saw us enter. Not till later did I learn that she would have felt disgraced if some other woman had seen me doing her work. Inside the

lodge I felt very strange, though I could not understand why. A young boy sat in there, naked except for a small apron hanging from his thin belt. His hair was tousled—cropped above his shoulders and in bangs across his forehead. His face was painted strangely and he was singing. Before him lay a small animal skin, turned so that its tanned side was facing upward and only a few whisps of dark brown fur showed along its sides. The boy was in the midst of drawing figures and designs on this skin, using small bones for brushes and beautiful seashells to hold his powdered paints, which he mixed with grease from a small bag. The figures and designs were made with many shades of reds, yellows, greens, and blues, blended so as to attract my eyes beyond my control for several moments. Meanwhile the fire crackled and blazed with the new wood, which the old lady was adding and the unusual odours of the place became even stronger as they got warmed.

This is my man, Stone Pipe, the Old Lady said, knowingly interrupting my prolonged gaze at his artwork.

He lives in a Dream World, though he seems to be here, she added, perhaps not meaning to confuse my thoughts so. Her explanations, right then, of the young boy were simply beyond my understanding.

In reply to my nervous statement of neccessity for departure, she thanked me for the assistance and asked for my company at supper in the evening, two days hence.

So, that is why I am going back today to call on the Old Lady and the young boy. Not knowing what to make of her statements, the other day, I have carefully avoided making any mention of her at the lodge of my Father, and no one yet knows that she and I have made any acquaintance.

.... The signs of evening are in the air as I make my way along the forest trail to get around to the far side of the Old Lady's tipi: Sun's light filters through openings in the dense growths of bushes, and Birds sing their Sunset serenades. Through the trees, now, I see their tipi, smoke rising from its center, curling up, and away, into the Air. Not far from the tipi—in front of the nearest tree—I see a fire, by a canoe turned over and propped up to serve as a shelter. The Old Lady sits smiling, before that fire; the young boy stands silently there. As they see me, the boy begins singing—in the distance there's an echo, somewhere.

Come, my boy, have a seat by this fire, the Old Lady says, as she beckons me near. *My man's Spirit tells him to be fasting, but two Fish for us he has caught. . . .I am now cooking*; and there, on sticks by the fire, I can see the pair.

The singing is from a boy's voice—high and gentle; but the song seems to convey wisdom seen with gray hair. Can a boy do such singing? I wonder—for the Spirit of his songs show great care.

I sit down by the fire—smell the roasting Fish, and the burning wood—see the firelight reflect from the grease and paint covered faces of the Old Lady and the young boy, see it throwing eerie shadows on the large Pine that looms behind us—practically over us. A sense of one-ness pervades the whole scene—a one-ness that I feel I am a part of—I want to join the boy's song; to stroke the Old Lady's hair; to melt myself like wax and pour myself among them.

Quietly, the Old Lady brings before her two wooden bowls. In each bowl she places a Fish and, from a small sack, a handful of dried berries. Without a word she gives me one bowl, takes the other and bows her head down in prayer:

HiYo you Spirits who are with Us: we thank you for this food—thanks for the Air; we thank you for our lives, and for the water; may we continue to be together, forever; and so, you Spirits, I end this prayer.

She lifts her head with a smile—a look of satisfaction. She sees me—as I am looking right at her—she gives a wink, with her left hand she smoothes her hair. Soon, busy eating, while the boy goes on singing, my thoughts are of everything there: of the People, of the camp, of my presence—of the Spirits that have guided me there.

We finish our meal fairly quickly, and clean the places where we sit. *Let us go into the lodge,* says the young boy, *let us go, for I feel another prayer.*

So we go into the tipi—the young boy leading. Behind me, the Old Lady brings the bowls and the foodstuffs; inside, she puts away what she carries and starts a fire in the center of the home. The boy, meanwhile, sits down on a pile of furs behind the center—across from where we entered through the door. He motions me to a place on the right side—to his left—where other furs are piled to sit on—a seat prepared.

My Mind often puts my words into prayer, begins the young boy, *and though my body has the appearance of youth—my Mind has before been in bodies—will again be in others, someday, somewhere.* I am not able to make any response to these words from this young man—I only wait—I know that something has brought me there.

The boy goes on: *Age, you know, is a physical thing confined to bodies—for the Mind is a Spirit and knows no time. If your Mind can be left free from your body—your life on Earth will seem like nothing compared to the Spirit of Minds that exist everywhere. Keep your Mind always searching—your Spirit happy. . . .*

A song comes from his lips then, as though it were still a part of the sentence *your Spirit happy. . . .* The young boy's eyes close—his mouth quivers, his face looks smooth and shiny—the song—the chant—goes on and on. I close my eyes—I release all of my muscles—I become detached except for feeling the songs flowing with my Mind. I float along, feeling musical colors—seeing sights of softness and beauty and an endless garden of colorful darkness. I hear his voice say—I hear an echo repeating: *My friend, I can see you with me there; and sure enough—as though in real life—I see a vision: I see the young boy as an old man sitting somewhere.*

I see you there, said again the young boy, this time with more emotion, *I see you there—yes, my friend—I'm with you there.*

The boy stops his singing and looks at me quite brightly—as though he'd found what he wanted in song and prayers. *Yes, you and I are truly brothers—the story's long, that's why you're here. . . .that's why you're here. Yes, once before you were beside me—another life time—another place—but you were there. Let my Old Woman, here, tell you how it is between Us, all.*

The Old Lady speaks: *Well, as I told you the other day, this boy is my man Stone Pipe—once with me while I was still quite young. I was his child bride—he was married to my two older sisters—when my parents were killed, one day while hunting—he took me in, made me as one of his wives. Before he left, he often said I should wait for him, he said that someday he would be back for his young wife.*

Well, continues the Old Lady, *he is here now, his body and his Mind, to help us All in our search for the highest Spirit in Life on this Earth. In the night, when we make love, we both find the Power with us—we feel the Spirit of those who are around Us, and those who were before Us. We hear the songs—see the colorful ceremonies, we learn to know them—for they can later help us to recall the Powers of Life that brought them to us in our Visions.*

So it is, says the boy named Stone Pipe, *that I am gathering together the powerful Bundle of Life. My strongest memories of those before me, and those around me come to me nightly—to direct and guide me—to give me Dreams which show me all the good Thoughts of Life.*

From long ago come the memories of my grandfather—how the People came to him in times of need. He would pray and sing his songs, and they left, smiling—for he had words that were of wisdom, come from devotion: to constant thoughts of happiness in All that he knew.

Sometimes my grandfather made use of certain things to help the People who came to him—to remember the Powers of the past, the present, and of All time. He used incense—many kinds—that All remembered, for many times they had smelled the sacred scents before, Way back in the days of our early ancestors the same kinds of incense curled their smokes from altar floors.

My grandfather always filled a pipe and gave his guests a smoke. It pleased him to see that pipe smoked all around. So I fill now this bowl with wild plants—we'll smoke with Nature. To our awareness of Nature's presence I will now pray:

HiYo Above Ones—You here on Earth, we seek to know you; you Underground, we ask that you shall remain strong. See that our Minds, like curls of smoke, can be united, with the vastness of the Spirit that's All around. Smoke with us here, Spirits, and let our thoughts be good.

With a stick from the fire he lights the pipe. He blows the smoke out, then he draws another breath in. Inside the bowl: the faint glow keeps getting brighter—a whisp of smoke comes up from it with every puff. Then on to me—to smoke the pipe—then the Old Lady—round and round, we pass that pipe, till All's smoked out.

My grandfather's proudest duty was the keeping of the People's Sacred Pipe Stem—all wrapped and bundled and kept from view by furs and skins of Animals. The Pipe Bundle—with its stem the length of a young child—hung above the Old Man, tied to a lodge pole. Every morning and every night he prayed before it—a prayer of humbleness to the Spirits which he knew were always present there. For, as far back as anyone could remember that Sacred Pipe Stem had been among the People—as a physical reminder of the Powers that have grown for Us, here, through the thoughts and prayers by All who Were, before. My grandfather often said that those whose faith was in the Powers represented by the Pipe Stem could do or have anything they really wanted simply by drawing on that Pipe Stem and thinking strongly about their wish!

Ah—is that not a powerful, wonderful thing—so much Spirit represented by one object. Ah—to capture some of that Spirit in one's Mind. . . .

. . . .Know you now, my friend—no, my Brother—know you now, that I am, here, the keeper of that Pipe.

Every night I pray before it, and see the People, the Ones, like I, who prayed to Spirits not in their sight. For now those People who were, before me, once with that Bundle, now they are present when All of the faithful pray every night.

Each night in my visions I see some Old One, doing something that is Holy, I try to remember, each night, that Holy sight. And so I'm learning the sacred ceremonies for my final: Bundle of Life. Shall I tell You about some of my Holy visions, my Brother? Well then, hear them:

In my First Dream—some while ago—came the call to gather: Bring together, come together, think of One-ness, said a voice from out of the depths of the Universe where was floating my Mind. Soon I saw them—a few old men—I watched them gather. They sang a song to give respect to Mother Earth:

> *This, where we sit, it is Powerful.*
> *This, Holy Earth, it is Powerful.*

I remember that song very clearly. One of the men then looked at me and spoke: Young man, You are chosen to help bring People together. We have not chosen you—no, You have chosen yourself, by coming here and believing Us. That is good—it will give you much happiness, this belief in our spiritual existence. We hope you will always believe in your Dreams, for they are guided by the Spirits with which your Mind dwells. You have chosen Us—our way is happy—it leads to goodness. Hear what we tell you, see what we do, remember it well!

The man who was speaking to me then unrolled a blanket and brought out the Old Sacred Pipe Stem—wrapped up in a bundle. He held it aloft, up towards Sun, and sang some songs, while he took the coverings off:

Man, you must say it, this Pipe it is powerful,
Man, you must say it, this Pipe it is powerful.

and

You stand up, you take me, you untie me, I am powerful,
You stand up, you take me, you untie me, I am powerful.

This last song sounded as though it was coming from the bundle itself, IT seemed to be singing, while the man untied the thongs and wrappings. Finally he brought out the Sacred Pipe Stem, which I immediately recognized as the same one my grandfather had, and that I now have. The man held the Pipe Stem before him, while its decorations of Eagle plumes—countless numbers of them—vibrated gently in the soft breeze. He prayed that Sun should yet become aware of the Power of the Universe and the Spirits of the Sacred Pipe Stem. And then he sang a fourth song—a chant, it was, without words—a tune so moving that each note seemed to beckon my Mind to join it on its journey into Space. While singing this fourth song, the man held the Pipe Stem close to him and danced in a slow circle, going first to the East and bowing, then to the South, the West, and finally the North. When he was finished singing and dancing he handed the Pipe Stem to the man on his left, who prayed with it and then involved himself in a similar dance. So it was with each of the men there, gathered in a circle in my Dream—each one prayed, danced in a circle, and bowed to each direction. The same song, meanwhile, filled the air.

Then the man looked at me again, and said:

Young man, we have now shown you the dance of the Sacred Pipe Stem—as it has been performed by countless generations of the past. You must remember and continue this ceremony, for someday a new generation will again be seeking the Old People's power—and this ceremony will inspire some of them on their way. You need not become a leader, or strive for power—for those who need you will come and find you anyway. Give what they ask for—tell them about Us, our ceremonies. If they should follow, and find new meaning for their lives by seeking Spirits, then you'll be happy, for their new strength will be in Your Life, as well as theirs.

Then the man reached inside of his buckskin shirt and pulled out a thin cloth bundle. He said, to me:

Sometimes it helps, while praying, to look at signs of the Universal Powers. While you pray in the morning, for instance, you see Sun's light—you feel warmth coming down to the Earth. After dark shines the face of Night Light—and of countless Stars that make the Heavens bright. In a storm you see the Clouds—you see the Lightning, you feel the Rain as it drops to the Ground. When you walk, you feel Earth—our good mother; when you swim you feel Water all around. When you pray you should think of All these Powers, let your thoughts make You, with them, feel as One. For All that IS makes the All into One-ness, and your prayers should bring that One-ness within you.

Now, young man, you have the Spirit of your Old People with that Pipe Stem, to be with you whenever You wish them there. But some of our relatives from the Bird and Animal kingdom, wish to be represented, too, when you make those prayers. In this cloth bundle is a whistle, for you to have—to help you with all your prayers. For when you blow upon its mouthpiece You will remember what you are seeing before Us All, gathered right here.

The man had pulled out the whistle and began to blow into one end, causing a high-pitched tone to come out of the other end. He blew softly, he blew hard, he made it vibrate, and soon some sounds in the forest we could hear. As he continued, the sounds continued to grow louder—soon many Animals and Birds joined our gathering there. In a circle, they stood around us—it was like magic—my Dream seemed real, like breathing in and out fresh air.

Here, young man, now take this whistle; take with you All the Spirits whom you've met right here, **he told me.** *Play your OWN tune, and always trust yourself to Nature, and All of Us will be with You, no matter where. We men, here, will come to you again in future Dreaming, so will our brothers, here, these Birds and Animals. Learn what we teach you—let your Dreams give you guidance. Now go—for Life is short, while with your body. Your new companions will be, from now on, with you on your Paths. Keep them in Mind with your songs and ceremonies, They'll give you strength to put in food for daily eating, they'll give you strength to feed your Mind during your fasts.*

And so, my brother, I obtained the whistle that I now keep with the Pipe Stem. I left that Dream down a new Path, with my new friends. Since I awoke they have been with me in my new Life—by day in thoughts, by night in dreams as strong as Life.

At later times I will tell you about all this dreaming, for later on You, too, will have dreams about which you can tell. Each of Us, here, at Hidden Valley, has dreams to guide us. We let that guidance decide the paths of our daily lives. We live by day what we dream in the nighttime, we let good thoughts and happiness be the dream of Our Life.

THE TALE OF SUMA, THE MUSICIAN

It is quiet this evening inside the community lodge—the families are all at home cutting up the meat from the day's hunt—shadows of meat strips hanging from strings reflected from all the lodge covers as I passed by them, on my way over here. Father was just tying more strings between the lodge poles as I left—three strings were already hanging across the tipi with drying meat.

Only Suma, the Musician, is in the big log lodge with me, now. He smiled pleasantly when I came in, and has been immersed in a slow song ever since.

Rrrrratt—rrrratt   rrrratt—rrrrat is the sound that is filling every corner of the otherwise-silent lodge. Suma has his big Music Stick before him—his favorite source of accompaniment whenever he sings alone. It is a branch from a Poplar tree, longer than a man's leg. Suma has carved the branch into an object resembling a knife, with large notches on the back of the *blade*. At the end of the handle is the carved head of his Medicine Animal, with beads and small bells wrapped around its neck. Suma has the point of the Music Stick on a piece of tanned Buckskin which is spread on the floor. He is rubbing a stick made from a Service Berry branch across the notches.

Rrrratt—rrrratt—rrrratt—rrrratt comes the sound from the notches as the stick bounces smoothly over them. . . .rrrratt—rrrratt—rrrratt—rrrratt. Suma is wearing his Buckskin suit with the red and white beadwork and the fringes of sewn-on Gopher tails. His hair is loose down his back, as it usually is in the evening, when he is singing. He is sitting, right now, on one of the low benches over against the log wall, away from the fire in the center of the lodge. I am sitting in one of the large chairs with the tree-limb armrests. It has a back and seat made from Willow branches. The lodge is comfortably warm from the fire inside the stone-edged pit. Water is boiling quietly in a kettle that hangs some distance above the fire—suspended from a steel rod that is also used for cooking.

Rrrrat—rrrratt—rrrratt—rrrratt, Suma's song goes on. He is singing some words, now and then, but I can't understand them. Mostly he just chants—the mood of his chanting is very strong and far-away.

O-WO-O-HO O-WO-O-HO O-WO-O-HO O-WO-O-HO-HE-JA-HE-JE-HE-JA

I close my eyes to listen to the song more carefully. Just as I begin to let my Mind wander up some grassy slope towards a forest, Suma stops his singing. He rubs his Music Stick a while longer, then he sets it aside also. He looks over here, at me, and continues with his pleasant smile.

You bring a smoke along? he asks me in a self-inviting way.

No, it's in my bag—over my bed. I can go and get it, though, if You want.

You no need to go, he replies, *is some smoke here, in the trunk with the Sesame Seeds. You smoke with me?*

Sure, I said, happily. What else could I say to a pleasant man like that? It is a real experience to be able to sit close by and watch Suma's pleasant face. I get up and sit on one end of his little bench.

Better you sit on the big bench by the fire—we have some tea when done with smoking, he advises. I oblige—the big bench has more room, and is further from the coolness of the floor.

Shortly he comes back with a little Buckskin bag—like the ones most of the People keep their *smoking* in. From inside his Buckskin shirt, somewhere, he brings out another bag—a little larger than the first—from which he takes a little stone-bowled pipe. The short stem has a carved snake twisted around it. The whole stem is smooth and shiny from being greased with fat, and reddish-colored from occasional applications of Sacred Earth Paint. Father's pipe looks similar to this one of Suma's. He fills the pipe, lights it, offers it, and we smoke—the firelight flickers and throws huge shadows of ourselves against the sloping log ceiling and the sturdy log walls.

. . . .Finished smoking—now drinking tea from gray, colored-with-age, tin cups. Tea made from Rose buds which the People gather in the Fall, just about the time of the first Snowfall. Father says the tea provides much nutrition during the Winter, when only meat can be gotten fresh. Songbird once told me that Rose buds are good for cold or fever if they are ground up and mixed with a meal, or taken as a drink. Suma has also brought over a dish with some Sesame seeds piled on it. They are good to grind up with the teeth, between sips of hot tea.

That was a Thought Song, says Suma, as though his singing had just ended. *Always gives me good Thoughts about near and far friends, and companions that I might somehow meet, yet,* he adds, as explanation.

One time I sing that song, sittin' in the afternoon Sun by myself, he says, as much to himself as to me, *I sure got myself some good thoughts, then—visiting with some folks I never knew before—never seen since.* I wait—quietly and patiently—while Suma stares into the fire. His pleasant face is still smiling—his eyes seem to be watching scenes in the flames that I can't see. He has introduced a story, and is now getting it together right. I say nothing—I try not to move. He may decide not to tell his story if he thinks I am impatient.

Was three of Us—three young fellows—walking along like partners, **he be-**
gins in a reminiscing tone. *Walking along in the Summer Sunshine—having
nothing to do but just to look around and see the living Spirits with Us. Everything was making Summer sounds of pleasure in Sun's warmth: Bugs, Insects,
Birds, Squirrels, Bushes, Frogs, all our relatives whom we can hear and see.*

*As we went along through the woods we came out into an opening and
found ourselves along the top of a ridge. We looked down below us and saw a
thin column of smoke rising from out of the trees on a point of land that went
out into a bay of water. We wondered who might be camping there, so we proceeded to climb down and see.*

*Was a lot of Brush on the way down—somehow I got separated from my
two Dream companions and was soon making my way through the Brush and
tangles alone. Up ahead of me I could see nothing but green growth, with the
column of smoke rising up from it towards the blue Sky above. For a bit I entered some growth so thick that I could barely even see Sky above me, then I
came out upon the bay's sandy shore. I looked all around, but there was no sign
of a camp or a fire, and I couldn't see the smoke column any longer before Sky.
Suddenly I felt very empty and alone, so I decided to sit down and wait for the
arrival of my two lost companions. I sat down in the sand—too soft, I think—
soon I was asleep, there on the shore of the bay....Dreaming....dreaming....
happiness....*

*....Water was splashing somewhere near me—laughing and giggling sounds,
I heard. Thought there must be some People playing in Water. My eyes opened
and I looked out at the water of the bay: a young girl was out there—standing
out in the water: bathing, laughing, giggling, splashing Water, she was. I felt like
part of the sandy shore—just eyes watching pretty girl bathing. Another girl
came to shore near the first one—layed down her robe on the Sand and waded
slowly out into the Water. Long, dark hair hanging way down behind on girl
wading out—now blowing to this side, then to the other...My eyes just looking,
my body all numb, like part of the shore. The girls splashed each other with
water, rubbed themselves with their hands—my Mind flowed out across that
Water to join them like a Cloud, it flowed away from my body in the Sand.*

As I watched, one of the girls dove beneath the Water. Then I heard some splashing quite near by—I looked to my right, by some Bushes, and saw the Sand  open up before my eyes. Suddenly, by those Bushes, there was a pool of Water, and a beautiful head came up from below—it was the girl whom I last saw diving, smiling to me, she said, "You are wanting to go?" So I quickly got out of my Buckskins, and got into that Water from the Sand. She motioned for me to come and follow, so I dove under with a tug from her hand. . . .

. . . .I found myself in a long water tunnel—the Sun light seemed to come up from below. With little effort I found myself drifting behind the girl who was swimming very slow. The silence of that Water was more than loudness, while the lighting gave everything a golden shine—like a dream was that beautiful, swimming body, going on as though flowing with All Time.

After awhile the other girl swam down to join us—she came up close, I saw directly into her dark eyes; then she turned and the two swam ahead together—I felt their water trail still vibrating, from the movement of their arms and legs and thighs. When our heads finally surfaced above that water, I knew we must be at about the place, where I first saw the girls join each other, from where they first caused my Mind to become dazed.

So we all three splashed water and laughed, and they still giggled, though the sound was more from pleasure than youth. It seemed so real—being in that water—part of Heaven. . . .just they and I, the Land and Water, and the Sky.

Slowly we seemed to play towards the shoreline, and soon we were standing by the robe. One of the girls picked it up with a laugh and began running, then we behind her, stepping softly in the sand. The warm air dried the water on my body, while locks of wet hair trailed behind from my head. Into a white lodge the girls kept on running, and when I entered they seemed to be asleep on a Buffalo robe bed. . . . .I went over and layed down between them, feeling warmth flowing all around—in that tipi with a blanket of Heaven, and a pillow of soft, warm Ground. I just let my whole self go, kept my thoughts on Sun, above—the girls were chanting, soft and low, while Everything on Earth made Love. . . .

The other day I was out on the lake Fishing—in my canoe—all by myself. I caught a few fish in the morning, which I tied to a braided Horse-hair rope and threw overboard. As Sun got near lunch-time I grew tired of Fishing—for some time I had caught no more Fish. So I got out my pipe and had a smoke, then rolled out my robe on the canoe floor and layed myself down. I looked up at the blue Sky above, and listened to the tiny splashings of water on the sides of the canoe, as it gently rocked to and fro. . . .

. . . .and I dreamed. . . .

. . . .The Fish on the braided Horse-hair rope were pulling my canoe along—we were headed across the lake. I felt like I was tied into the bottom of the canoe, and I could not get up. I just laid still and looked up at the Sky and listened to the water splashing off the sides of the canoe. Finally I was able to sit up—just as I heard a nearby sound of rushing water. I looked ahead and saw that my canoe was caught in a swift current that was heading for a huge rock-faced wall. I grabbed for my paddle and tried to control the canoe, but it was of no use. Just before we reached the rock wall I noticed—looking over and through the waves which were rising and falling all around me—that all the water was rushing into the opening of a cave that barely showed above the water level. Quickly I laid myself back down and called on my Guide to protect me. . . .

Whoosh—sh—sh—sh Tush—sh—sh—sh. . . .the sounds were like many waves breaking on shore during a heavy storm on the lake—I dared not look— several times the canoe jarred against boulders and other solid objects, and each time fear made my muscles tighten and my heart call a halt to its beating. Yet, in no time. . . .

. . . .silence. . . .

the sound of the rushing water quickly faded into the background; I raised myself up to look around: I was on a large, green lake that stretched as far as I could see, and was dotted by many islands—one of these was nearby. I noticed that I was sitting in water, and a hole in my canoe's bottom caught my eye. I had nothing with which to bail the water, so I took my paddle and worked furiously to reach the nearby island's shore. The beach of the island was level and smooth, and the water before it was calm. I was almost up to it when my canoe gave a final start and dropped out of sight below the line of the water. I was able to stand up on the lake bottom, and the water felt very warm. I took hold of the Horse-hair rope and dragged the canoe along as I waded into shore.

Once on dry land I dropped the rope and continued my walking. The smooth sandy beach went inland for half of a mile; before it ended where some low cliffs rose abruptly, hiding from my view whatever was beyond. I reached the cliffs and climbed up through one of the rain-washed gullies that looked like a tiny canyon in the mountain of sand. If I had hopes of finding food or shelter, on the other side, I was soon disappointed. The cliffs were like a solid sand wall that only enclosed another body of water—a lake within a lake. I hiked back to my canoe and sat down to ponder my fate. . . .

. . . .stranded on a strange island with only a sandy beach and nothing to repair my broken canoe with. . . . . . . .when I heard again the sound of rushing water—this time only briefly before the sound was replaced by that of a water spray—and it, in turn, by the sound of countless drops hitting the lake top. I looked up to see a most gigantic fish floating at the top of the water—its eyes and back and part of its tail sticking up in the air. At this sight I became very much afraid. . . .

. . . .but the giant fish spoke to me, in a deep, gurgling sound that was more comical than fearsome. . . *My friend, have you a light to make a fire?*

I have my flint and steel, sir, I answered hesitantly, *but it won't work in water.*

That is all right, said the large fish, *for you may light my pipe for me on the shore.*

At that I saw an object floating towards me across the water—shaped like a pipe, it was, and it was headed ashore. I drug the thing out of the water—it had a stem as long as my leg, and a bowl as large as a kettle. Inside the bowl was a tangle of leaves and vines that looked like an uncut salad. I was surprised to note that all was quite dry. The large fish spoke again:

You must light my pipe and offer smoke to the Spirits. After that float it out here to me. When I've smoked I will be able to help you—now, go ahead, strike your light and make my smoke.

So I reached into my own little tobacco sack—its contents all wet from my adventure—and brought forth my little waterproof bag made from a Rabbit's intestine. I unrolled it and brought out flintstone and steel. To the top of the pipestuff I put a pinch of moss-fuzz. With the flintstone I struck the steel in my hand. The spark flew, right away I started blowing, and the pipestuff began to crackle and burn. To the mouthpiece I ran, in a hurry, but to draw on such a pipe I had to learn.

The mouthpiece was huge—at least by what I was used to. I was not able to suck air through a stem of such length, but I found that I could blow down the stem to the pipe bowl, and the weight of its contents was not disturbed at all by my breath. However, the pipe stuff was soon heavily smoking—like a campfire just doused with water from a large cup. While the bowl rested securely in the soft sand I moved the long pipe-stem all around—I pointed it, first, to the Four Directions, then held it upward, and finally down, towards the ground. Once more I blew some of my breath down through the pipe-stem, to make sure that the stuff was well lit, but a breeze came and forced the smoke down the stem and back out at me—and right down my lungs it did hit. . . .

. . . .I tried to lift myself back up from the ground—I could see nothing, for the smoke still hung around. The sandy Earth felt like smoke—into which I kept sinking—I relaxed and something lifted me Up to my feet.

Be careful, my boy, that stuff will get You, said the big Fish, *that's from a good crop—I picked it from the deepest part of the lake. I dried it there, on that shore—an old Crow helped me, all seven days he slept and dreamed, while wide awake. But where I keep it that's my own secret—I can not tell You, but I can help You find finer places, here on this lake.*

The large fish instructed me to push the pipe back into the water. I gave it a light shove and let it float to where he was. I quickly did as he asked me, while I wondered: Where would he take me? What would I see? How would this end?

For awhile he smoked his pipe occasionally blowing streams of water up into the air—while he looked off across the big water to I knew not where. Then, all at once, the pipe was gone, his eyes were gleaming, he half sang out: *Are you ready?* Then he swam close up—I swam to meet him—I got aboard him. His big, tough wrinkles gave my feet a real good grip. I stood above him while he propelled us through the water. Like a fast canoe, we went along, but without the strain of paddling. A warm breeze made my braids float behind me—into the Air as though to join the Birds that flew around. A flock of large ones was nearby circling—what kind they were, or where they came from, I never found.

I used my bow to keep my balance while a fine spray of water tingled my body—bathed in Sun's light—that light came like a River from behind soft clouds—sometime to go yet, before would come again the night.

As we went along we passed by close to some islands—one, two, three; and at the fourth one we stopped. With a jump I was back in the water, a few strokes, a little wading, and I was back on solid ground.

If You should need me, after I'm gone, said the big Fish, *just stand in this water; take four big mouthfuls and spit each one as far as you can. I will come to meet you, smoke my pipe, and try to help you; but next time I do that, is the only other time I can.* With that he swam away, and I was sad to see my new friend go. Yet, I knew that his life was quite unlike mine. While I live upon the Earth and not the water, his home—the lake—gives him the stuff to make HIS life just fine.

When the big Fish was gone from my sight I looked around the shore of the island. There were footprints in the wet soil everywhere. I looked forward to being, again, with other People, and hoped that they could help me on my way.

I followed a path which led through the willows, that grew in a moist hollow close to the shore. A cutbank surrounded all but the water-side of the hollow. The path went up and over the lowest part of the cutbank and into a light forest of bushes and tall shrubs. The path led along, through several small clearings, till it finally came out to a meadow of good size.

In the middle of the meadow was a strange lodge like I had never before seen. It was long and low—quite different from the lodges we use here. A Person, stooped over, was just going inside. The back of the Person's robe was brightly decorated, and the colorful art made me feel much at ease.

I approached the strange lodge, wishing someone were outside—I grew nervous at the thought of having to go inside announced and seeing all the occupants staring at me. From the sounds of voices and other noises which I could hear, I knew that a number of People would be within. I walked up to the door while two Dogs watched me closely, I looked in the door and my heart skipped a beat. I couldn't decide on my first reaction as I saw the strange gathering there, ahead of my feet. A number of Persons were seated in that lodge, some with most hideous faces. Someone said, *Come inside,* and as I went in they all rose and offered me their places. At the rear was a man who was surrounded by smoke, and he motioned for me to sit beside him. I was brought up to respect the meaning of the place beside the host's seat that is offered to an honored guest, so I went to the rear and sat down. I forced myself to look at some of the other People in the lodge, out of courtesy, but I was careful not to focus my eyes upon them. I was afraid of myself, what my expression might be, if I dwell-ed on the thought and the meaning of this group—if I rested my eyes on their physical appearances.

I am Smoke Head, said the man beside me in a thin, strained voice that sounded far away. *Did Huka, the Fish bring You to our island just recently, or have You been lost?* he asked.

I have just arrived, said I, quiet-ly so as not to attract too much atten-tion to our conversation. The others in the lodge seemed to have forgotten about my presence very quickly, and were again involved in their own visits and chores. *I came here hoping that you would be able to give me some assistance to get back to my People,* I said, very hopefully.

Of course we will assist You, said Smoke Head, *that is what We are All Here For, don't You know?* He seemed to imply something that I could not figure out. He continued to smoke constantly, his head being barely visible, at times, inside the cloud. Strangely, the cloud of smoke stayed only around him, and seemed to rush immediately upward and out through the roof opening, with-out affecting anyone else in the lodge.

May I spend the night here, with you People, before setting out on my journey home in the morning, I asked, confidently. Everyone's hospitable man-ner had made me feel very much among helpful friends.

Certainly You will spend the night Here, replied Smoke Head. *We will know when You are ready to go home.* For a moment I thought that in his efforts to make me feel welcome he was inviting me to stay with them for a visit. His following conversation, however, added quite a different light to this idea than I had expected. He said:

All of Us are Here to learn some Lessons—to understand different things we never understood before. Some People on Earth think others' Lives should be in their power—they think that Power means having control of others' lives. When they do this they get sent here, to our Island of Purgo, to live with their own power, feel its evil, and cast it out. If they do this then they go back to re-arrange their Earthly ways, after their deaths their Minds will live on in Universal Happy Days. But if they cheat, and try again to control another's destiny, their Minds will forever dwell in misery!

My own fault is that I am immensely fond of smoking, so much so that my Mind always seems clouded up, and I am never quite sure about what I am doing. I harshly criticise others without knowing the pain I may be causing them, be-cause the smoke reddens my eyes so I can hardly see. But here, the others pay no attention to me—all my bad thoughts stay in the smoke around my own head.

When I go back to my Earth home I look forward to looking around myself—to speak to others, to find out their desires. My days I'll spend with others, sharing happiness, to make my smoke filled with good thoughts during the night.

Smoke Head ended his conversation with a moment of silence, followed by a mighty siege of coughing. After awhile he tapped my knee and said: *See those two ladies with the funny heads?* as he pointed out two women down the way. Both had spooky faces that nearly frightened me, and one had a strange growth on her head.

Back at home they are known for their gossiping—everyone always says they have big mouths. The one talks a lot about just everything, the right one pries a lot into other People's lives. All day long, now, they just sit there gossiping, while no one here pays them any Mind. Pretty soon they will see the ugliness in each other, if they're left alone, then they may try just to be, again, good wives.

Come outside and I'll show you the Frog Chief, he's the one who gave everyone commands. All day long his loud voice disturbed the peacefulness, as he shouted his orders through the camp. We walked out of the lodge and I was greatly relieved—the place was just too strange for me. I still wondered for the reason of my presence there—I wasn't like them—that was easy to see.

There is that Frog Chief—in his water hole, when he shouts only croaking can be heard. He is finding that life goes on around him anyhow, even if he doesn't say a single word. And there, in a small water hole near the lodge sat the strangest frog I have ever seen: a feather in his long hair, a pair of earrings, a Chief's arrow that his odd fingers held between. His croaking sounded funny, the way his face appeared, as though he were shouting in vain. I could see how obnoxious he could try to be, but as a Frog his Spirit gave me no pain. I hoped, for his

sake, that he could learn to keep quiet, now, and that, with silence, he would still have the same strength. Where words can add little to others' Spiritual needs, actions can often raise them to great lengths.

Let me show you the three brothers who are un-happy now, said Smoke Head, as he led me through the field. *One had more success than the other two, so the two tried to have the third one killed. Their brother is still at home, but his Spirit's here, to show them what might happen if they pro-ceed—with their selfish plans to take his happiness—like robbing a good hunter of his meat.* And there, down below, I could see them now—two sorrowful runners being chased, by a laughing, huge skull that kept behind them right along, now and then tapping their backs with its bony face.

Next thing I knew I was walking away from them—leaving those weird People and their strange lodge. They were waving, making strange sounds, till I lost sight of them—as I hurried back to the water and, I hoped, home. I waded out and took four mouthfuls of water; I spit each one out, just like the Fish said I should do. . . .then I woke up and found myself in my canoe!

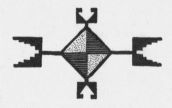

Get up, says my father, splashing water in, *you're lucky the Wind blew you this way. Some others, in the past, went fishing like you, today, and they got lost in some faraway place. They've re-turned, telling stories of strange People there; a hid-den and magical race. They came back, very frighten-ed, from whatever they had seen. It must be power-ful, whatever it was that they had seen, for they came home and changed their Paths to better ways.*

So speaks my father, here at the shore, as I wake up. I'm not sure just what to tell him so I'll just think: Make others pleasant, before seeking my own pleasures; avoid ugly gossip—tell things about others right to their face; don't shout orders or use words for what You can do better—let actions take the place of spoken words; don't think evil of others who have what You want—be happy for them and they may show You their ways; and, finally, think carefully about all your dreaming—let it be the mirror of Your Mind throughout your days.

DREAM OF THE GIANT

The brother of Father is visiting with us this evening. *Uncle Big Snake* we call him. A handsome man in his 70's. Uncle Big Snake is good to look at while he accents his story telling with hand signs. His shiny, brown forehead goes some ways up where his hair has receded, while his silver-gray locks fall to his shoulder behind. He is telling us now:

Once I dreamed I was in a very strange place: all the natural things seemed to be the same as here, in the Valley—the trees and mountains and streams—but all the signs of human life that I saw were very large—several times larger than they usually were. I came upon a place where some tall trees had been chopped down—apparently to make firewood, or else, perhaps, a shelter. The trunks were all gone—only the stumps were left standing. Yet, all the remaining stumps were two or three times as tall as I—there was enough useable wood left just in these trunks to supply most of our camp with a Winter supply. In addition, more than a Winter supply of firewood, for our camp, was scattered about in broken branches, left by whoever had taken the trunks.

I looked around me on the ground and noticed some very large depressions— large enough for me to lay down in. Walking around them I discovered that they were in the shape of footprints—huge footprints, they were! Following the direction the footprints were leading—first with my eyes—I saw a path clearly ahead—a wide swath of crumpled bushes and broken small trees, as though a landslide had here finished its downhill run. Yet, there were no piles of Earth or large boulders—just those huge footprints sunk down into the ground.

I was amazed and curious—not yet afraid or angry—so I followed this trail of destruction to see where it would go. I had not picked my way along the tangled trail very far when I came upon the carcass of a Deer. It appeared to have been butchered, but only one hind quarter was actually gone—other parts were just lying about, while most of the animal seemed to have been torn and shredded as though someone had hacked around on it with a hatchet. As I look- ed more closely I noticed several pieces of sharp flint protruding here and there from the body—each one as large as the blade of a knife, but somehow driven into the body without any handles. Other pieces of flint were scattered about, some of them were stuck in a large pine tree behind me. The tree's life-juice of sap was already oozing out.

I continued to follow the tracks to a stream bed, where whatever it was must have stopped for a drink, for at the water's edge I found the remains of the hind quarter, and in the warm air it sure did stink. One footprint was left right in the water, and the creek, at that place, flowed out upon the ground—in a hundred small branches it divided, and everything was muddy, all around.

I went on, and up ahead I heard loud noises— from some bushes were coming loud sounds. I approached with my bow and arrow ready—I expected a huge Bear, ready to pounce. But—oh! how I shrank back with horror when I saw what was making all the noise: it was a man of gigantic proportions—a huge man with a bellowing voice:

"What brings you here—you weakling—you servant. . . ." as his huge hands reached out and grabbed hold of me. . . . "Come with me—I'll find use for your presence. Can you cook well? Can you chop down a tree?" Though he asked questions he must have thought of his own answers, for he never gave me a chance to speak. He just roughly threw me into his big basket, which from filth and contamination did reek.

Outside, I could hear him laughing loudly, and at times he seemed to be grumbling some song—he was rising, and planning to take me along.

"Another warrior, perhaps, I have captured—another weakling to fight my enemy's men; seven hundred he has killed, of those I've sent against him; there'll be no peace until for every one I've killed ten!" So I heard him talking, then loudly grunting—but all the odours made me feel pretty weak. He swore loudly about stepping into something; he kicked the basket, and I fell on my cheek.

A sudden updraft brought fresh air into my basket, as he took my conveyance upon his back; His steps and bouncing sent the basket swinging madly, and, oh! how the forest did crack.

I found a loose piece of the basket to hold on to, and, for the first time, had a chance to look around. The basket, to me, was quite a big one; and through the space between the basket weavings, I could see, way below me, the ground. A nearby sound suddenly caught my attention, and I noticed another person by me; he was covered by loose leaves and branches—it looked as though he were sleeping, to me. He sat up and looked at me sadly, then he asked, "Have you been here very long?" I shook my head and said, "Just a few minutes," and he told me, "You should have never come along."

It turned out that he, too, had been captured, and he knew what our fate was to be. He said, "Two giants are at war with each other, and for fighters they use captives like you and me."

I asked him where the two giants were living, and he told me on opposite sides of a lake. "They lived at one time together, like two brothers, but then each wanted more than he could take. So they fought, and threw words at each other, and each one claims that the other is bad. They're too busy making war on each other to notice that All around them is sad."

My companion-in-plight told me how the country has suffered, since the giants have lost all common sense—wrecking forests, killing game, and cursing Nature; using innocent little People for their defense. I asked him of the Deer that I saw earlier, and he told me how the giant kills with flints—"Instead of using one accurate arrow, he throws a handful, quite blindly, at what he wants. He often hunts when his stomach is filled up, so he takes only what he sees fit. At his rate there will soon be no Nature—his desires fall into a bottomless pit."

I asked my friend if there was any way, now, that we could save each other's life. "Not a chance," said he, with a look of dejection, "Not unless we can find us a knife."

Well, then, it did just so happen, that my knife was still tied to my side. We took it and started quietly cutting that basket till we fit through it, and dropped quietly outside. The giant just kept right on walking, his noises covered any that we made. My friend said that without his two captives, the giant would find his war hard to be made.

So, in my dream, we gathered my friends' People, we had them move near my own People's campsite. The giant was quite upset at the desertion, for, without them, his existence soon died.

THE THREE FAMILIES

There once lived three families whose members were all close friends—they lived as neighbors, and were happy together. The men hunted and smoked with each other, the women cooked meals and sewed clothes together, and the children went hiking and swimming together. They shared each others' joys and sorrows, and they helped each other with whatever they had.

So they lived, until one day one of the women, looking up, saw an Eagle of exceptional size and beauty flying overhead. Though she had no particular need or use for the feathers, she said—aloud—"I would certainly like to have the skin of that Eagle."

After some little while one of the other women, looking up at the cliffs nearby, saw a herd of Mountain Goats. Though she had plenty of skins and furs in her lodge, she said—aloud—"I would certainly like to have the skin of such a Goat."

The third woman, after thinking over what the other two had said, saw a beautiful golden Snake sunning itself on a boulder nearby. Though she could think of no use for any part of such a creature, she said—aloud—"I would certainly like to have something from that beautiful Snake."

Now, the three men of the families were sitting nearby, smoking. They had heard what each of the women had said and, though knowing that the statements were made from idleness and had no meaning, they each said—aloud—"I am able to fill my woman's request."

So, the men went off to climb the nearby mountain—one looking for the large Eagle, one for the herd of Goats, and one for a golden Snake. They found the Eagle, first of all, quietly nesting. As they approached, the Eagle asked what it was they wanted and, when it learned the intent of their mission, it asked them to come near. From its tail the Eagle gave each of them a few feathers and said: "Your People shall always wear these to remember the power of the Eagles—you may return home, for that one woman will now always have Eagles dropping feathers in her hair."

So, the men went on to find a Goat skin. As they neared a herd of Goats, one old nanny came forward and asked them what they wanted and, when she learned the intent of their mission, she asked them to come near. She gave them each a fine suit made of Goat skin and said: "Your People shall always wear such clothes to remember the power of the Goats—you may return home, for that one woman will now always have Goats rubbing their fine fur on her body."

So, the men went on to look for a golden Snake. As they came to some boulders they were startled by a loud hissing, and shortly they saw some gigantic Snakes coming near. The Snakes hissed and shouted at them: "You came for us, but yet you stand there with cold fear. Your People shall always fear Snakes,

when they see them, and all they will get is a good run for their lives, because of our power—you may return home, for that one woman shall have plenty of Snakes curling around her feet, now!"

So the men ran home, now rather frightened. From a distance they saw their three tipis, but none of their families seemed to be about. As they came closer they found only some piles of their clothing and their footprints that showed where they had gone: in the background, where in the past only flowers had been standing, stood three pine  trees, tall and dark. From the one flew an Eagle, losing feathers, on another a Goat had rubbed its hair, and the thrid one had Snakes that were coiling in the Sunshine by its roots, upon the ground, everywhere.

SAVARO—THE MAKER OF THINGS

For several days I have been hearing the distant tap-tapping of Savaro's tools while he has been making a new canoe from the trunk of a large tree. I have seen him, from a distance, sometimes working alone, sometimes working with the help of one of the other men in the camp, or even with the help of his woman, Raspberry. Savaro and Raspberry live in a large log house covered with Earth, which they built on a knoll by the shore of the lake. Savaro did not want to build too close to anyone else's home because, as he once told me, *only I can enjoy the musical sounds of my tools as they help me to create all the things that I think of.*

Whenever I see Savaro around the camp he always asks when I am going to come by to see some of his creations. Today I will take advantage of his invitation, so that I can also see how it is that a tree trunk can be turned into a balanced canoe.

Hello, do you have a few minutes to visit, Savaro shouts eagerly from a distance as I walk down to the edge of the lake where he is working on his canoe. It is a warm day, and he is taking advantage of the weather by letting his skin feel the air and soak up Sun's rays. He has a strip of buckskin tied around his head to keep his hair back, and a black beard covers most of his face.

Our house is a little out of the way, so we don't get visitors too often, he explains with a large smile on his face. *Hey Raspberry,* he shouts in the direction of the house, *make some tea—we have company.* My visit seems to have aroused much enthusiasm within him.

Little Bear and his sons helped me to haul this huge tree here, he says, pointing to the canoe-shaped hulk before him, *after I felled it with the use of various tools. I've been hollowing it out with my chisels for a couple of weeks, now, and I'm just about ready to try it out.*

I build small fires in the parts that are hard to chisel, though I have to watch carefully that the fires don't burn too far into the side. Today I've been using my planer to smooth the surfaces and make them even. I use a fire for this job, too, if a large area needs to be leveled. I just run a torch back and forth along the high spot, and then I scrape it off after it has been scorched well enough.

I guess I can leave this go for awhile—I'd like to show you our house, he says questioningly. I tell him that I'd love to see it, and he eagerly guides the way along a winding, stone-laid trail that takes us up the knoll and into a clearing in the growth of trees, where sits the large Earth house.

It doesn't look very high, but mighty big, I comment as we approach a small vestibule with a door, which is a part of the house.

Oh well, wait until you see how it is built inside, he explains to me, as he opens the plank door to the ringing of many strands of shells that are tied to a bouncing willow stick which is fastened to the inside of the door. A strong accumulation of odd and mysterious odours rushes for the door as we step into the vestibule. Coats, shoes, and caps are hung on the vestibule wall, while various wood and Birch-bark containers stand in rows on the floor. Another doorway—without a door—leads into the main room of the house, which is several feet lower down than the vestibule.

You see, the house looks low from the outside because it is actually partly underground, Savaro explains triumphantly. *This knoll is exposed to rough weather from across the lake,* he goes on, *so we stay pretty snug and protected way down here. Besides, Raspberry and I feel real secure living down here in our Earth Mother's womb!*

We spent a long time digging out this pit and making it level. Then we lined it with logs, which we continued above the ground for four more feet, before laying the logs across to support the roof. I fitted the upper parts of the walls so that there were plenty of openings for windows, which is why it looks so bright down here. Don't you think it's bright down here? he asks hopefully. Indeed, it is a very cheery home that actually gives no indication of being partly underground unless you look out through one of the open windows and see that the bottoms of the nearby trees are about eye level. The floor space inside here must be four times that of a large lodge in the camp—at least thirty feet in each direction. A large, colorfully woven blanket hangs across a far corner of the building, making a triangular room behind there. I have been hearing noises from that area since we came in, and now I find that it is the sleeping section, and Raspberry is just arising from a nap. She looks startled to find us in the house, but immediately joins the conversation.

How are you—how is everything in the camp, she asks. Before I answer she continues, *have you seen Savaro's new canoe? He's been working on it for quite awhile now, and expects to finish it very soon.* She seems to be fully informed about his activities and eager to tell someone else about them.

Why don't you make us some tea from those roots you dug yesterday, Savaro suggests to Raspberry. *I want to show our guest some of the things we have around.*

Some of the People in the camp scoff at me because I'm always working with tools and building things. They think I should spend more time just wandering around and daydreaming. But this is my life, right here—that's what I do the best and what I enjoy doing the most, he says, while making a sweeping motion with his arm to take in all the contents of his home. *Some of the People called me Tool Man, sometime ago. I told them I didn't care much for that name, so then some of them started calling me Not-Want-To-Be-Called Tool Man,* he said, with sort of a puzzled look on his face. *I'd rather be called Savaro—or else just plain Neighbor. I mean, we're All neighbors, aren't we?*

Where did you get all these odds and ends, I finally had to ask. The ceiling beams are just covered with hanging things like pieces of chain, metal rings, big skeleton keys, parts of old guns, and numerous things that I don't think I've ever seen before.

Ohh—just scavenging around, he replies, acting somewhat as though I'm prying. *It's really amazing what stuff you can find around the old trading post—stuff that got lost and broken. I don't figure anything should be left to waste if there's a chance something can be made out of it; everything's got some use to it, if it's handy when you need it.*

Here and there I see baskets with Food, bowls with dried plants and herbs and mysterious little bags. They must sample many of Nature's things. In the center of the house is an open firepit with a waist-high wall made of rocks. Raspberry is pulling on a rawhide rope that is attached to some sort of a pulley at the edge of the fireplace. Soon a clay vessel comes up from the fire and, as she pulls on another rope, swings out to the edge of the firepit. *I rigged this thing up so that we can control exactly how fast our food cooks over the fire,* Savaro explains. *This other rope lets us swing whatever is cooking out here, to the side, so that we don't get burnt leaning over the fire. I made these bellows,* he goes on, pointing to an affair on the floor that has a wooden foot-pedal, attached to another rawhide rope which hangs from the ceiling beam, above. A folded leather bag is fastened beneath the pedal. *I made these bellows from a tanned Elk hide that I soaked in Bear grease, to make it air-tight. The rawhide rope has just enough give to let me push this pedal down—as soon as I take my foot off it comes right back up to place. When we get up in the morning all I have to do is toss a few sticks of kindling into the ashes, here, and pump on the bellows for a few moments, and the fire starts up. The nozzle from the bellows fits into a hole that I left when I made the stone wall, around this fireplace. I can pull the nozzle out and use the bellows for other things—such as providing the air to play this harmonica that I found the pieces of,* he goes on, pointing to a strange object that is roughly the size of a harmonica, but is made mostly of smoothed and polished pieces of wood. One side has a leather cover constructed so that a round piece protrudes, big enough to stick my thumb into. *I just put the nozzle of the bellows in here,* he points to the protruding round piece, *and pump the bellows. To play a tune I just cover different holes up here, in the front. I'll show you.* He fits the nozzle of the bellows into the hole on the harmonica cover and pumps the bellows with the instrument's other side. Horrible squeaking sounds can barely be heard above the puffs of air from the bellows. *I told Suma he could have this when I get it*

perfected, he says, *but Suma doesn't want to carry too many things around with him when he wanders, I guess. He said it would be better if I learned to play it—then I could maybe accomapny him. I've tried talking Raspberry into learning to play it, but she says she doesn't have enough time.*

Savaro lays down the bellows and harmonica as I walk over to a massive workbench along one wall of his house. *By the way, I use the bellows and fire-pit to do a little blacksmith and jewelry work, too,* he adds as an afterthought. *Every once in awhile somebody brings me a piece of rock with some workable metal in it—some Copper or Silver—and I make them bracelets or a ring or, some earrings out of it, in exchange for what's left over. With the bellows and a good fire I can work with a lot of metal—though I really prefer wood.*

 *Here is your tea,* says Raspberry, as she brings over two wooden cups of steaming liquid. *I hope you like it; Savaro and I like this kind real well,* she explains. We sit down on a bench made from half of a log, with wooden stems for legs. The tea is dark reddish-brown in color, and smells like something in a pharmacists collection. It has an odd taste that I can't describe, but it is pleasant to swallow. Savaro takes out a little Buckskin pouch from his back pocket and a small, clay-bowled pipe. *Would you care for a smoke,* he asks, as he fills the bowl with tobacco from the pouch. *I call this smoking mixture my Tops and Stars, because I made it from the smallest and softest parts of my smoking plants—the parts closest to the warmth of the Heavens above,* he says in a reminiscent tone. *The Summer's End Ceremony will begin pretty soon,* he continues, *and with it we'll have our harvest. Here's to a good crop of every-thing,* he calls up, as he points the mouthpiece of his small pipe towards the Sky. He puffs on the pipe for some time before passing it to me. Raspberry shakes her head when I try to pass it to her. Taking the pipe from me Savaro explains, *naw, her head's up in the Clouds most of the time, anyway, she doesn't like to have smoke floating around her, too.* He chuckles quietly, while Raspberry assumes a look of having her head up in the Clouds.

We sit quietly for awhile, feeling the warmth of the afternoon through the windows nearby. *Would you like to go back outside,* asks Savaro, apparently feeling also the beckoning of Sun's rays. I nod and get up, handing my empty cup to Raspberry with a smile of thanks. She smiles, in return, and continues to scrape at some wrinkled, brown roots with her knife, up on her cooking counter.

Outside there is a warm vibration—an almost-silent sound of brightness, warm air, Birds in the Trees, and countless insects busily at work in unseen places. Savaro walks to the edge of the knoll and sits down on a huge stump that he has evidently moved there himself, as it just sits on top of the ground like some giant's footstool. I sit down on the stump, by Savaro, and there is yet room for a couple more People to sit. The view out on to the lake is most overpowering from this point. Like a huge, blue mirror, it reflects its frame of green forest and high, rocky pinacles. To think of the World which exists at the bottom of that lake, alone. Fish, Plants, and Insects living together in an environment so much different than the one up here, yet so much in Harmony with it.

Do You see that little island out in the middle of the bay, over there, asks Savaro. *That's going to be the next goal of my Dream Life. I want to build a small version of my Earth Lodge over there. And I'm not going to use any tools or metal things there—just for the Experience of doing it that way,* he says. I am trying to picture a small Earth-covered lodge on top of the island.

The trail down to the water, in that bay, is a real steep one, Savaro goes on. *You see, the whole bay is surrounded by rocky walls that drop off straight for a hundred feet or more to the water. I figure that even if People from that World Outside ever find their way to our Valley, they're not going to be very anxious to disturb me out on my island home!* He gives me a sly wink at that.

I'm going to try to pack whatever supplies I'll need over there in along the frozen lake-top this Winter, he continues, still looking over at the island with a dreamy film over his eyes. *Then I can hike in and out during the Summer at my leisure—depending on whether Raspberry and I like this place better than that one,* motioning to his present and future homes with his chin.

Are you planning to use your new canoe to reach the island, I ask.

Yeah, he says, in a far-away voice, *and to explore other parts of the lake from there. That reminds me,* he says, in a sudden tone, looking towards his canoe, *I would like to finish smoothing down the inside and outside of that thing today. Would you care to give me a hand?*

There are still several hours left to the afternoon, so I'll go ahead and help Savaro with his canoe. I'll just leave my clothes up here, on this rock. They would only get in my way while trying to work in this warm air.

My grandpa used to do a lot of travelling in a canoe, Savaro informs me. *He came over here from France and traded with different groups of People for furs. He'd load up a big freight canoe with trade goods like knives, axes and beads, and paddle several hundred miles upstream, trading on the way. When he had his canoe filled with what he wanted he just drifted back down to where he started out. When he got older he went to work for the factor at this trading post, and married his daughter. So, you can see that I am related to Two Crows, whose great-grandfather was that factor. Quite most of us are related here, by now, and the subject has caused some concern among the People in the camp, I know. They're worried about the future. Let me tell you a story about the First Canoe, as my grandfather used to tell it to me:*

STORY OF THE FIRST CANOE

A tribe of People made their homes on the West side of a wide river, far from these mountains, here. Every Winter they would migrate to the Plains to hunt Buffalo and bring back their hides to tan during the Summer. They crossed the River toward the East, and came back West, to their land, before break-up in the Spring. At the end of one such Season of hunting a young man, his wife, and his baby son fell behind the rest of the tribe as they were moving back to their country. The young family had brought more Buffalo hides than they could conveniently carry, so they were forced to travel very slowly. Now, by the time this family reached the banks of the wide river. break-up had already started, and they were no longer able to cross. They sat on the bank and mourned over the situation that they were left in.

While the man and his wife were so mourning, and their child was crying along with them, a Coyote came along, floating down the river in a carved tree trunk. This was back in the days when the bodies of animals still looked pretty

much like those of the humans. This Coyote saw the mourning People so he floated his craft over to them and asked them why they were so upset. The People told him how they had gotten stranded on this side of the river because their heavy Buffalo hides had not let them travel as fast as the rest of their People.

Now, Coyote had an idea. He said to the People: *This body that I have does not quite suit me. I float along this river with my carved tree trunk, but I am not wise enough to make any good of this travelling. No Animals will have me in their camps because I am too much like a human. Yet, no humans will let me come near because my face is that of an animal's.*

Since my face looks that way, it would be best for me to just be an animal. So, if you will give me one of those fine robes that you are packing, man, then I can cover the rest of my body with fur. And if I may have one of the braids of your hair, woman, then I can unbraid it and wear it behind as a tail. And if I may learn your mournful wail, young child, then I will have a sound that will make all others pity me. In exchange for all this, I give you People my carved tree trunk, for it shall be of no use to me, anymore. You can fill it with your things, and float it over to the other side, and join the camps of your People.

And so came the first Canoe to the People, says Savaro with a knowing look. And we let our Minds wander to those long-ago days of Animals and Humans, when they were learning how to get along with each other. . . .

THE HUNT

From a deep sleep I awaken to hear someone talking quietly into my ear. Startled momentarily, I look up to see my Father smiling—looking anxiously at me.

It is time for the hunt! he says, when he sees that I am awakened.

Ah yes! Now I remember—the hunt—this morning we are to go for a hunt. Fresh meat to add to our meals of fine vegetables and berries—fresh meat to give our bodies strength—hides for the women to tan and sew into things—sinew for sewing—hooves to carve children's toys from—scraps for the dogs—and. . . .the Spiritual Adventure of the hunt itself!

I pull myself up to my elbows—my fur-robe-covering slides down and exposes my chest to the damp morning air. I feel good—looking forward to the warmth of my clothing. My hair is tangled and my mouth feels as though still asleep—but, shortly, I am up and have my clothes on, my hair brushed, my mouth rinsed, and my face and arms washed with cold water—my skin feels alive with a stinging warmth underneath the security of my clothing.

By the fireplace sits a bowl of grain-meal, which Father is now and again dipping his fingers into, as he leans his head back and opens his mouth. I do likewise, throwing the meal into my mouth with gusto, fiercely chewing up the grains and dried berries, and then swallowing each mouthful down to feel the new activity in other sleeping parts of my body—which are now waking up and making me feel even warmer—and stronger.

I sit down at the edge of the blankets and furs that make up my bed and I put on my moccasins—folding the tall flaps firmly around my ankles and wrapping the long thongs several times around them. I tie my knife sheath to my belt—the blade was just sharpened last evening while we all sat around the fire, talking—and I tie a rolled-up scarf around my head to keep my hair from falling into the way of my eyes. From the rope that holds up the tipi's inside lining I untie the

thong by which hangs my bow case and quiver and their contents. Proudly, though just for a moment, I look at them: my own bow and arrows—made by the hands of Savaro, that bearded, magical craftsman who lives with his woman and his work in an Earth-covered lodge, over on the other side of the bay. A strange man whom everyone likes, but no one really knows. I look forward to visiting with him.

While I was admiring my fine hunting gear, Father has stepped outside and, from the sounds that I hear, he is preparing his Horse for the ride. Quietly, I stand up, pick up my bow and attachments, and lift aside the Elk skin door covering—looking back, momentarily, at the still-sleeping occupants of the lodge, all looking so comfortable, so warm—giving me a warm feeling inside.

Outside: the air is much more damp and chilly than I expected—the moisture on the blades of grass looks cool and gray. I hang the bow and arrows over my back—the strap across my shoulder. I learned some time ago to wait for this part of dressing until outside—after getting outside the lodge once or twice and finding my bow and arrows stuck crosswise inside, between the lodge poles on each side of the door.

Father is mounted now, and ready to go. I hurriedly slip the main piece of my hackamore over Matsoaki's nose, pull her ears through the neck strap, untie the rope around her foot (she makes a couple of meek efforts to have me leave that rope by lifting her foot up), throw the reins back over her head, and leap smoothly up on her back. She is restless from her night of standing and doesn't want to hold still while I get a proper hold on the reins and make better my sitting position. I give her just the faintest nudge with my heels and she immediately tenses her hind end and makes an effort to leap forward and take off at a gallop. I check her with the reins, and we move quietly away from the big, red-painted lodge. No one else in camp seems to be awake yet, which makes it hard for me to decide whether this is the very end of yesterday or the very start of today. I dwell on that. . . .

The mist in the air gets thicker as our trail takes us into the forest—it looks more like fog, hanging there among the trees. At times Father is far enough ahead of me, on the trail, that the details of his figure begin to fade into the mist that he appears to be continually riding into. The Horses' hooves make squishy, thudding sounds as they pound down upon the dark, damp Earth. We ride in silence while the morning light slowly dawns on us and, bit by bit, makes more of the details of our surroundings become visible to my eyes. We cross a tiny, rushing stream, and pause to let the Horses suck up some of the water. Suddenly: in the woods—there's a CRACK!. . . . Matsoaki halts her drinking immediately and lifts her head several inches—her ears turning one way, then the other, water draining from the sides of her mouth back into the creek. I hold my breath to listen, but I don't hear any more sounds. The Horses finish drinking, and we continue along the trail—all of us giving expectant glances into the trees in the direction of the sound. . . . CRACK! There goes the same sound again—followed by silence, as we come to a dead stop in our trail. Father looks carefully, then gives me the signal to get down from my Horse. Silently I dismount—lifting one leg over Matsoaki's back and sliding my body down her side, opposite from where the noise came from. Father is tying his buckskin gelding by the front legs with a long thong, which we both carry for that reason. I do the same.

I believe there is an Animal in that brush just off to our right, he whispers in calm words. My breath, by this time, is coming in short gasps, since the excitement has mixed with the cold. *I will go around to the other side of the sound and give you the Owl call when I am ready. Then you may enter straight into those bushes, as quietly as you can, and one of us, at least, will see what is making that noise. . . .*and he is away, silently.

I do not need to wait very long to hear the faint *Ooh-Hoo, Ooh-Hoo*, of Father's voice. I have gotten my bow out and slipped the loose loop over the notched end. Now I get out two arrows from my quiver, mount one, and hold the other one with my bow hand, parallel to the bow. Picking each step carefully, between small brush and occasional branches, I advance into the bushes where we last heard the noise. . . .on and on, the distance passing slowly with such careful steps. Suddenly: like an explosion of brush and animal, a large shape bounds out just a few feet in front of me and away in a straight line. . . .the main thing I can see is a large white tail, waving in the air like a flag in the hands of a nervous flagman. Two or three long bounds the beast takes, covering distance so fast that I don't even get my bow into shooting position, much less aimed for a most difficult rear-shot—when up jumps Father, about one bound ahead of the Animal, with his bow drawn and ready. Only the top half of his body is visible in the tall grass where he has been hiding—he must have known just about where

the Animal was and suspected its route of travel. The twang of the bowstring is almost immediately followed by a light, thudding sound. A twitch in the Animal's body signifies that the arrow has found its mark. Yet the Deer—a large white-tail, it turns out—continues with its long bounds and is shortly out of view inside the next bunch of bushes. Father holds up his hand, motioning for me to stand still, so I listen: a loud crashing sound has followed the last sound of a jump, and now the crashing sounds become general, as though the Animal is rooting and thrashing around in just one bush. . . .then there is silence. Father remains still for a few more moments—I do likewise—then he heads in the direction of the last sounds, drawing his knife from its sheath as he walks. By the time I catch up to him he is pumping the Deer's hind legs, forcing the blood to run out of the opening in its throat which he has made.

My brother, it hurts me to do this, he says, towards the Animal's body, *but my family is in need of the food which you will provide for us. I pray that your Spirit continues to dwell here and that it may be good for those whom you will serve.*

Having said that, Father begins to open the animal up with his knife so that he can clean and prepare it. He looks to me and says, *You may as well go on ahead without me. I will prepare this Deer, here, and then pack it back to camp. If you have not arrived back in camp by mid-afternoon I will come and find you. Continue down the trail we were following, and turn to the left at the first fork that you find. In a short distance your trail will drop down into a small clearing— stay at the edge of it and you may be able to observe some feeding Deer or Moose. Sometimes they bed down in the thick of the brush, there.*

I nod my understanding—at the same time sweeping my right arm away from my stomach, as Father often does when he means, *It is well.* I walk back out to the trail and untie Matsoaki's feet, and jump back on top of her.

I head Matsoaki down the trail as Father suggested, and soon we come to the fork, where I head left towards the mountains that form a high, solid wall on that side of our World. Looking over the tops of the trees ahead, where they appear to be downhill, I can see a light area that must be where the clearing is that Father mentioned. I dismount and tie Matsoaki's rope to a solid, old stump, just off the trail, that sits by itself and has no brush or other trees near it. There she can find a bit of grazing without being able to tangle her rope up in any growth.

As I continue on foot the trail makes a sharp right turn and then drops downhill, as the trees thin out, away from it. At the bottom of the small hill I can see part of the clearing—covered with low, green bushes, green grass, and numerous white and purple flowers. What a breathtaking view:

The width of the clearing is equal to the length of a tall Pine Tree. The ends of the clearing are hidden from view by the forest at my right and left. On the other side of the clearing, straight ahead on this path that I am standing in, begins the thick, dark forest again. It lays like a continuous carpet, in all directions. It ends more than half-way up the mountains which loom over this clearing with immenseness. Above the line of the forest can be seen the bare slopes of the mountains—large boulders strewn here and there along the paths of old slides. A few of the high-up ridges have green tree growths on top of them—like hairy moles in the faces of the mountains. The mountain which is somewhat off to my right has a sheer cliff of red and yellow Earth facing my way. The lower reaches of the cliff's face are lost somewhere in the green forest below it. Patches of white, here and there, represent the remnants of the one-time glacial covering of these mountains. And above all this the Sky forms a bright blue backdrop to an everchanging pattern of clouds that seem to rise up from the top of the mountains and flow this way—as though they were being brought to life by some magical power just behind the high peaks above us. If I let my eyes dwell on the clouds for a few moments I get a strong desire to reach up and touch them. . . .

After looking over the clearing and inspecting the paths and tracks, some of which are quite recent, I've picked a spot from which I can remain best hidden while still able to cover the most likely parts of the clearing. I'm seated on my blanket at the edge of the trail that I came in on—just a short distance above the main part of the clearing. I brought over some broken Pine branches and built a simple wall that will hide my movements and presence from the eyes of any game which might be inspecting the surroundings before venturing out to graze in the little meadow. I've made a few trial sightings, and should be able to reach most of the meadow with my bow from right here.

Sun is well up in the Sky by this time, and the air is warming up—so much that I might as well unbutton my shirt. A contemplative smoke would go well right now, so I might as well bring out my pipe and fill it. My small travelling pipe and its bag are fastened to my quiver. I untie the knot in the tie string and unwrap the mouth of the bag. I pull the little bag open at one end and pull out the short wooden stem with its wrapping of sinew. I reach into the bottom of the bag and bring out the little, black stone bowl, shaped like a small elbow and polished till shiny with grease. I fit the tapered end of the wooden stem into the smaller of the two holes in the bowl and draw on it, to see if the passage is clear. It is. Again from the bottom of the little pipe bag I bring up a pinch of my smoking mixture. I put this into the larger hole in the pipe bowl—the one with the black crust around it that gives off a sweet smell from many smokings. I tamp the mixture down with a twig laying nearby me. . . .

. . . .I awaken with Sun shining hotly upon my face from its middle-of-the-afternoon position in the still-blue Sky. For some time I have slept—dreamt of the Earth and all the things upon it: the Pebbles and Twigs, the Insects and Flowers, the Birds and Animals, the Sky up above. I have been as one with them in my dream—I am as one with them, lying here, waking up, on this warm afternoon. I take my shirt off to feel the faint breeze uniting with the moisture on my body. My face feels hot and tingling from lying motionless in the path of the hot rays for so long.

The afternoon breeze brings with it an overpowering sound, out here in this mountain forest—a sound that is the voice of everything which is around here—a HUSHhhhh—a visible sound in the tops of the nearby trees as well as an invisible droning that seems to be coming down the canyons and mountains and through the forest from the vastness above. Leaves rustle; twigs snap; an occasional tree trunk groans as if passively greeting the rush of the unseen air or commenting upon the burden that it must continuously bear.

I will have another smoke from my pipe, while deciding whether to remain here or to get up and wander around, in order to locate the object of this hunt. I knock out the cold ashes left in the bowl from my earlier smoke. I fill the bowl with another pinch from the bottom of the pipe bag, and tamp it down again with the same twig, which still lies where I last tossed it. I wonder what will become of this twig after I leave this place—for I will probably never see it again.

I must cover the match well to keep the breeze from blowing it out. I must marvel at the ingenuity of that Savaro—making these matches from twigs, Pine sap, ancient gunpowder, and sulphur from the cave of an abandoned early-day mine. Though all the People in the Valley take with them their flint and steel, when travelling away from home, these matches are a great convenience when one only needs a quick fire like this. . . .

. . . .Big, gray whisps of smoke drift away from the top of the pipe bowl and out from the corners of my mouth. The heat from the burning mixture stings my tongue and warms my mouth. Slowly I puff—blowing the smoke out and watching it rush off with the breeze—mingling with it to disappear into the Universe.

Suddenly! I am consciously aware of some sounds that my subconscious Mind has been making contact with for some little time—occasional sounds somewhere out in the forest—sounds like twigs breaking and brush rustling. . . . I listen silently—Silence! Just the Wind in the mountains and down here in the trees. Silence! Then! There are the sounds again—sounds such as would be made by a child quietly playing with sticks inside of some dense bushes. Couldn't be a Person—though the sounds seem much too strong to be any small Animal. A large Animal, then—what kind? I wonder. . . .as my heart begins to beat faster and my hands begin to feel moist and tense. Again, I hear the sounds—as though they seem to be a bit closer each time. The sounds are coming from the brush on the other side of the clearing and some ways off to the right. But I can not see a thing moving.

Quietly! I remove my bow from its case and gently place one end against the instep of my foot—bending the other end so that the center of the bow bulges outward. I pull the loose end of the bowstring up towards the top notch of the bow. I almost have the loop over the notch when the whole affair breaks loose of my nervous hands—the bow almost propels itself into the air as it straightens out. Luckily my hands have enough of a grip to keep this bungling silent. Again I bend the bow—this time more quickly so that the loop is over the notch before my hands can lose their grip again. I take four arrows from my quiver and place three of them in front of the bow, where I can hold them with the same hand as the bow itself. The fourth arrow I lay in place, carefully fitting the bowstring between the notch. I hold the arrow in place with the index finger of the same hand which holds the bow and the other arrows. Using my right hand for support I raise myself up very slowly and quietly. . . .

. . . .I almost lose my balance getting up—I am dizzy from being on the ground so long. The sounds now seem to be fairly close—yet I can still see no movement in the brush, nor any other sign of the noisemaker. I wonder if it could yet be some very noisy small animal?

I am carefully making my way down the trail toward the clearing—each step is a studied and measured one, so that my presence will not be announced.

During my smoking I noticed that the gray whisps went hurriedly in a direction away from the clearing, so my scent should not make its way over to whatever is making the sounds. Ahead lies the upturned trunk of a dead Cottonwood tree—an ideal shelter for me to make my stand behind. I lean myself against the trunk to rest my body from the strenuous few steps it has taken.

There! The tops of some tall bushes are swaying unnaturally—that must be the location of my quarry. Like a chain-reaction in slow motion, the movement in the tops of the bushes comes slowly towards the edge of the clearing, over on the other side. If the maker of the movements continues in that direction he or she will step out into the clearing almost directly across from me, a stone's throw away. A chill rushes through my body, and I wish I had kept on my shirt—to help silence the loud beating of my heart, if nothing else.

The bushes at the very edge of the clearing are swaying now—and I can barely make out some dark object through the many leaves. Suddenly! The quarry steps out into the open—so defiantly that it must not have any awareness of my presence. It is a Moose—a large, dark cow Moose with an appearance which makes it look almost awkward: a large head at the end of a massive neck, which ends in a large hump above the Animal's shoulders. A monstrous nose hangs almost comically at the end of the cow's face, and a little, dangling beard hangs under her chin. She is huge—about the size of my Horse Matsoaki, though some of the huge appearance is due to unusually long legs. The cow's hind parts seem small and incomplete when compared with the massive front. She stands still, as though waiting for something to happen, and I begin to raise my bow into position to shoot. . . .

. . . .Crack! More of the sounds which I was hearing for some time, though the maker of the sounds seems to be standing silently out in the clearing. Crack! Crack! And out from the bushes comes another Moose—a powerful-looking Bull with his weapons of horn adding a great deal to the massiveness of his head and shoulders. His shiny coat of hair is almost black, except down around his feet, where he seems to have on golden-yellow socks. His tiny eyes seem inadequate for such a large body and, indeed, I have been told that he relies on them much less than his nose and ears. He does not seem to be concerned about any possible challengers—he appears to be very relaxed. Few beings in Nature would dare challenge such a monstrous combination of legs, horns, and muscle.

The cow begins to wander along the edge of the meadow in a direction away from me. I was hoping that they would come this way, to give me a closer and more powerful shot. I will have to aim carefully and shoot quickly if I am to have any success with this challenge. . . .

. . . .Thummmmm—goes my first arrow, the bowstring snapping sharply against my wrist. The cow stops and the bull doesn't move—not a muscle. Quickly I fit another arrow to the bowstring and pull it back—I must hit him this time, though I felt sure that the first arrow hit the mark, also.

Thummmmp—goes my second arrow, making a definite sound of striking its mark. The bull twitches his body once, but otherwise stands still. I fit yet a third arrow to the bowstring and start to pull it back when the bull turns—and begins to trot towards me. I aim carefully below the swaying hump on his back—long, black hairs bristling noticeably on its top.

Thummmmp—goes the third arrow, its feathered shaft protruding over the bull's big ears. He makes a momentary lurch, then halts in his tracks. I fit my last arrow to my bowstring—the others are deep in my quiver which hangs on my back. As I fit the arrow the bull begins to trot towards me again—though much more unsteady than at first. He is now close enough to be on fairly intimate terms with me. I can clearly hear his labored breathing, which only adds to his apparent ferocity. I aim again below the swaying hump—hoping to strike some vital area underneath. It is the only clear shot that I have from this head-on position.

Thummp—goes the fourth arrow, striking harder and more quickly than the others. The big bull crashes to his knees as my heart skips a beat. The feathered shaft is barely left sticking out from his back. His shiny eyes have a look of disbelief as well as a look of conviction to do harm to this unexpected challenger who looks so weak, standing there before this ruler of the forest. With loud, labored breaths he again begins to rise. I quickly pull the quiver from my back and reach in for more arrows—dropping the quiver from my hand as I fit one of the arrows to the string. The battle will shortly be over—but the big bull is not yet ready to accept defeat. He still has left enough power to take me with him on this last physical journey. With a few more steps he will be upon me. . . .

I begin a song—a loud song of courage for myself—an announcement of victory—a demand for his acceptance of defeat, and I let fly another arrow.

Thumpppp—the arrow goes deep into his side, which he has left barely exposed to me. Crash—the bull goes down on his side. His legs make an effort to lift the big body up once more, but the damage which has been done is too heavy to lift back up. He raises his head in defiance, looking about for me in his last attempt. I let go of another arrow—this one deep into his heart from very close range—and he drops his head with a last sigh. My song continues as loudly as I can sing it, while the tears run from my eyes and fall to the Earth below. I feel badly for ending the life of this powerful being; I feel badly, and in my song I tell him so....

HiYo my Brother—forgive me for doing this to you. Let Your Spirit always be with me in exchange for this physical ending which I have caused. Give spiritual strength to all those who will strengthen their bodies with you. HiYo-HiYo, HiYo-HiYo!

Go now, woman, I find myself shouting-singing to the cow, *go now, for he is mine. You would not have stayed with him long anyway—another will find you and take you soon, in this forest.* The cow will not listen to me—she challenges my right to her slain man's body as she stands as close to him on the other side as I am standing from him here. She snorts loudly, and paws the Earth with her large hooves. *Go,* I shout again, waving my arms at her, *go, or I shall have to take you with me as well.* I have one arrow left, which I fit to my bow, fearing that she may attack me. I do not wish to shoot the cow, if possible, for she may give the forests many young bulls, yet. Again I shout at her, *Go, go from here—your man is mine now,* and as I wave my arms and my bow she begins to retreat, stopping now and then to snort loudly—a snort which echoes menacingly from the trees around the meadow. All of Nature is watching this powerful Drama of Life.

With my knife I take care of the first part of the operation which will end up providing many meals for the People at home. It is a tedious operation, which must be done carefully so that nothing useful is damaged or ruined. I leave my bow case and quiver lying by the big bull, to keep away any hungry Bear or other marauders, while I go back to Matsoaki to ride her down to the camp. I will need the help of some others to bring this massive food supply back home....

Night is half-way over by the time I take a plunge into the cold waters of the creek, where they flow out into the lake. We have finally completed the job of hauling my success of the day back to camp and hanging it from the branch of a tree out of reach of the camp's Dogs—hanging it so that it can cool and mellow naturally. As I am cleaning off the labours of the day, it is hard to believe that all this has happened in just one day—how dramatic can be the events of some days!

SUMMER'S END CEREMONY

Early in the morning it is, again—finally the start of the day on which is to begin the Summer's End Ceremony, which we have All been anxiously awaiting. Songbird is walking around the camp with some bells in his hand, which he keeps regularly ringing. His deep, penetrating voice can be heard all over the campground loudly proclaiming the spiritual event that is to take place on this day. Now and then he calls out someone's name and reminds them of the duty that he or she is to fulfill for the ceremony.

Arise, my friends and neighbors. . . .arise, all my relatives, here, he is now saying. *This is the first day of our Holy Season—this is the day on which we start our Summer's End Ceremony.*

Hey there, my young friend Two Crows! It is for you to take along some boys and gather the material for the sweat lodge, which you must have built by this afternoon. Send a boy out to gather some fine rocks that will heat well. It is for you to decorate the insides of our Holy Lodges—to make the Earth altars and decorate them with Earth paints and feathers, so that they will be ready for the incensing during our ceremonies.

Hoka hey, my friends, hoka hey! Let Us be moving along now—let us make ready for the busy day. This evening will be the first ceremony inside the West lodge. When Sun sets our food will be roasting over the firepit inside that lodge, and we will all gather in there, at that time, to partake of the food.

Okeh, my friend Little Bear! Are your boys getting up and making ready for the work of today? You will be bringing the firewood to the West Lodge, and covering its framework with those grass mats and lodge covers that are in the storeroom. Tonight you will be singing for the Owl Dance, which will be bringing this day to a close many busy hours from now. Let's go! Let's go!

Good morning, all you women! Help to get your men started so that everything will be ready this evening. We're going to have a good time together— happy days, Holy days. Hoka hey! Bring your berries and meat to the Camp Hall for cooking—let us have a good feast tonight. Hurry up! Hurry up!

Someone pulls aside the door curtain and calls to me, interrupting my involvement in the wake-up song that Songbird is loudly in the midst of. It is Two Crows, looking in.

Can you help me with my work, he asks. *I have sent someone out to gather the rocks for the sweat lodge, and I will send out another young boy to cut the willows. I would like you to help me in putting the sweat lodge up and in preparing the altars and Holy lodges. Will you come?*

Yes: yes! I'd love to—perhaps you can teach me some things about the ceremonies, I eagerly reply. Since Two Crows is a man younger than I, I will be able to ask him about things that are not proper to ask the older man with whom I visit.

Two Crows is waiting outside, sitting on the ground in the early morning Sunlight, whistling quietly to himself. Other People in the camp can be heard talking, coughing, and singing, as the households prepare for the day. The new baby in Low Horn's lodge is having its wake-up exercise of crying while its parents are probably trying to get themselves ready, as well, for the day. As soon as I finish braiding my hair I will be ready to go with Two Crows to see what is to be done. None of us will be eating anything until the feast this evening. We are getting ourselves prepared for the four days of fasting, which will begin after these first four days of the opening ceremony.

Two Crows is still whistling as I step out through the doorway. The camp has a feeling about it—a vibration—of many Spirits coming together for some major event. The lodges look particularly bright and cheerful—not an unhappy note anywhere. Songbird has mounted a Horse and is now riding around the inside circle of the camp, still singing his songs. He is dressed in all manner of elegant plumage—looking like a proud creature of the Forest and Mountains, parading before his peers. A headdress of black-tipped Eagle feathers covers his head, tufts of Horsehair floating away from each feathers' tip. White Weasel skins hang from the sides of the strip of quillwork which seems to join the feathers together over his forehead. More Weasel skins hang from the arms and legs of his Buckskin leggings and shirt. The smooth looking Buckskins gleam shiny yellow in the bright light—partly because they have been rubbed with a light-yellow colored Earth that is found under a cutbank by the far side of the lake.

Some use the yellow Earth to paint their faces, others color their moccasins and even their tipis with it. Songbird has painted his Buckskin suit with it, simply by rubbing it gently into the grain of the hides. He has a bead-embroidered martingale hanging over the shoulders of his favorite Buckskin-colored gelding—small bells jingle from the ends of the tassels at each side. A number of People around the camp circle have paused to admire the Old Man as he gaily makes his rounds on the Horse—a colorful and glistening sight that gives Us strength and inspiration.

Let us go over to Little Bear's and see if one of his boys can go out and cut the willows for us. We can, meanwhile, gather some firewood and prepare the ground around the lodge, says Two Crows, while we walk towards the lodge of Little Bear. Inside the lodge several voices can be heard singing a slow song, while others inside are making various sounds and noises getting themselves ready. The songs are being practiced for the Owl Dance, tonight.

Hello Father, says Two Crows respectfully to Little Bear. *Can one of your boys help us for a short while to obtain the willows for the sweat lodge,* he asks. Little Bear smiles and looks around at his boys, of whom there are several. His wife cheerfully volunteers the services of Horse Rider, their youngest son, who is braiding a long Buckskin rope that is tied to one of the lodge poles. She says to him, *You go and give some help to these People, what they are going to be doing is very important. Us older ones have to get that West Lodge all ready for tonight, and you would probably just be in our way there. Here, you take along this big knife of mine—and be careful that you don't cut yourself! You'll be needing that if you're going to go and cut all those willows.*

Work well, says his father while giving him a pat on the shoulder. In a moment Horse Rider is out of the lodge and walking along side of us, acting like a pony that has just been let out of a corral. Two Crows tells him what he is to do, and he listens very carefully: *We need one hundred good willow sticks for this sweat lodge,* he explains, *for a Holy sweat lodge must be strong, and it must be large enough to have room for many People. Get straight sticks about the thickness of your fingers, and twice as tall as you are. Trim the leaves and branches off where you find them, so there won't be a mess here in the camp. We will help you to cut the last four—the big, long ones. Now go—we will be in the middle of the camp circle preparing the ground. Bring the sticks there.*

Horse Rider heads for the trail which will take him over to the point of the small bay, where there is a dense growth of willows on the shore and some ways out into the shallow water. Two Crows, meanwhile, is leading us over to the storeroom to pick up some things we will be needing for our work. Two women are just leaving the storeroom with some of the camp's cooking gear—including a large brass kettle and a metal tea pot that is as large as a bucket.

Inside the storeroom everything is cool and quiet. The storeroom is actually a large building made from massive Cedar logs. A heavy door made from rough-hewn planks is the common way of entering the building, but there is also a double set of doors—one set on the inside and one on the outside—that are suspended from sturdy runners. These open wide enough for eight People to walk through side by side. The lighting inside is dim, but covers every part of the building. It comes in through numerous small window openings that have been placed around the log walls. A thin-scraped sheet of rawhide covers each window opening and is well tacked down all around, to keep out air, moisture, and smaller visitors who might wish to take up living among the stores, there, and eat up some of what is being carefully preserved.

The building is a maze of framework, inside, on which rests a great variety of material stacked in many separate layers to allow air circulation, Two Crows tells me. Some wooden canoes rest upside down near the ground. A dozen, or so, wooden spoked wheels are stacked nearby. Numerous boxes and crates line the floor space, while countless tools and implements hang from thongs fastened along the walls. Two Crows walks over to a section of farming tools and takes down a heavy metal rod—one end sharpened like the point of a spear. From a suspended pole covered with thongs and laces he takes a handful of thin leather strips.

Now we can start, he says as he heads for the doorway, *we will come back here later to get some other supplies.* I close the latch of the heavy door and hurry to catch up to Two Crows as he walks to the center of the camp. From one side of the camp is coming Horse Rider—already carrying a bundle of cut willow stems.

Every year we build a new sweat lodge, says Two Crows, as he locates the place that we will work. *We take down the old one when the ceremony is over,* he continues, *and make a new one to be strong enough to hold all in camp. We make our family sweat lodges from the willows when this lodge is taken down.*

First I will dig the hole for the rocks—you can just watch me for a few moments, he tells me, as he begins lifting out pieces of sod with the pointed shovel. He is taking each shovelful to a place that is directly East of where he is digging. *This will form the Sacred Mountain of Earth,* he explains about the place where the sods are being piled. *This Holy lodge is so large that I must dig four holes—each of them will be filled with red-hot stones, in order to thoroughly heat the lodge up.*

In just a short while Two Crows has finished digging the four holes—all of them equal in size and round in shape—*to represent the roundness of the Earth and the Universe,* he explains. The Sacred Mountain is quite large, now, and Two Crows tells me, *we will prepare the Mountain later on, before the ceremony.*

With a long stick Two Crows carefully traces a line in the dirt—a large oval that goes way around the four holes which he just dug. Handing me the metal rod with the sharp point he says: *You make the holes in the ground, along that line, while I sharpen the willow stems and cut them the right length.* He tells me to make the holes about the width of my foot apart from each other. There will be very many stems making up the framework of this sweat lodge!

As I proceed around the oval with the metal rod, driving it down as hard as I can, pulling it out, and driving it down again, Two Crows follows me. He inserts the sharpened end of a willow stem in each hole that I dig, and soon we have a small corral of upright willow stems, the ends of some are waving in the breeze as they point their way up towards the Sky.

Now he brings forth the small bundle of leather thongs and asks me to bend one of the willow stems from my side into the center. He bends one the same way, from the other side, and we tie them together with a thong where they meet. This we must do to all the parallel willow stems, until we have a long, arch-like framework over the marked out area. . . .

Two Crows has gone out and cut the eight main willow stems—big, long ones that are used to tie the lodge frame down length-wise. Four of the big stems are put into the ground at each end, then bent toward the center and tied together. Next, we tie the long stems cross-wise to the many short ovals, to make the willow framework very solid.

The rocks have all been brought beside the lodge by the boy who was sent out by Two Crows earlier. Some distance directly out from the doorway of the lodge Two Crows now digs another hole—quite a large one. Together we start a fire in it, which Two Crows tells me to tend while he goes to the West Lodge and scatters Pine branches on the floor and arranges the altar in back for tonight's gathering. I have to begin putting the rocks into the fire when it gets hot enough. . . .

Sometime later in the afternoon the People begin gathering at the sweat lodge, bringing with them their robes and some other hide or mat to contribute as a temporary covering—for the length of the Ceremonial Days. Two Crows has sent some boys out to gather armloads of Sage, which he is spreading over the sweat lodge floor. The rocks are all glowing red inside of the big, hot firepit. As soon as Two Crows finishes with the flooring, the People begin crawling through the doorway and finding their seats inside the lodge—men to the right and women to the left, and children with their mothers or fathers. Two Crows and I stay behind to pass in the many rocks—four sets of four fist-sized rocks are placed in each of the four pits inside the lodge.

Hot air comes drifting out of the lodge—hot, burning Air. The People pass out their robes, which we lay in two piles by the sides of the door, before we enter the lodge ourselves. After the door coverings are tightly pulled in place we find room for ourselves and sit down. The Earth beneath our bare skin feels cool and damp compared to the heat and dryness of the air around us.

Songbird sits at the rear of the lodge, two large Eagle wing fans in his hands. The four rock pits look like underground lanterns—red eyes of the Earth. Everything in the lodge is illuminated by a deep, red glow. The tanned bodies of the People fade into the dark lodge coverings behind them, but the whiteness of their teeth and their eyes gleams brightly all around. Songbird begins singing: *He-Ja, He-Ja-Ha. He-Ja-Ha. Hey-Ja-Ha: He-Ja, He-Ja-Ha, He-Ja-Hi-Yo.* . . . His Grandson, Dreaming-of-Elk, is sitting near him in front of one of the rockpits, takes up the tune in time to the dipping of four cups of water, which he splashes on the rocks before him. *Tushhhhhhh. . . . Tushhhhhhh. . . . Tushhhhhhh. . . . Tushhhhhhh.* is the sound of the meeting of those Powerful Elements—Water and Fire. Clouds of steam rise up from the rocks with each splashing—up to look for an escape into the Air above. Finding only the lodge's thick coverings, the steam clouds billow out and begin to engulf the lodge's occupants, who are still bathing in a red glow. Sways-with-the-Wind sits at the next pit after Elk. He is a shy young boy, so his singing can barely be heard above the voices of the other two, and the splashing of water on the rocks that are before him. More steam rises into the Air, and hangs over us like a nighttime fog. Good Man is next in line, and he joins in the song and splashes water. His rocks sizzle and pop, and he smiles with satisfaction, as the steam spurts upward.

The song ends after four cups of water have been splashed on the rocks in each of the pits. For some time we all sit quietly, barely being able to breathe the thick, wet air, and feeling the sweat running along the skins of our bodies as though we were in a shower. Songbird signals for the curtain to be opened, and a number of People crawl outside to sit in the warm, fresh air for a spell. The steam pours out through the doorway and soon the inside of the lodge is cool again. The others come back in, and we start the singing and steaming again. . . Four times we do this. By the fourth time I can't tell anymore whether I am inside or out, or how many others are still present in the lodge. Some of the People have remained outside after the first or second round—especially some of the women with children. Now the rest of us go outside and rush over to the mouth of the creek, where it flows into the lake. Amid sighs and loud *Ahhh's* all the People jump into the knee-deep water and lay down, to feel the coolness of the creek passing over their bodies. I close my eyes and put my head under water, facing upstream, I feel like I am falling through endless Space after I let go of my hold on the weeds growing at the bottom. My knees scrape the bottom and I regain my Earth-consciousness, as the current has flowed me to the edge of the lake. I get back up on my hands and knees and gasp for breath, my head just above the water's surface. I have to stand up to breathe as full as my lungs demand—though I almost pass out again while getting up. Hardly a word is spoken by anyone, as the People continue to bathe, or sit at the water's edge and gaze out across the lake, or wander back up to their robes by the sweat lodge. . . .

Not long after the sweat is finished the People all gather again—wrapped in their robes and seated in their places inside the West Lodge. The lodge looks like a tipi that was cut in half and had two parallel walls placed between the two tipi halves. It is built on a framework of tipi poles, and covered with several old lodge covers and numerous mats made of Tule reeds woven together. Along the top runs an open space that lets us see the Sky and allows the smoke from the fire within to escape. The fire is built in a narrow pit the length of a man. The women are preparing the meat which has been roasting over hot coals for part of the afternoon—choice pieces of Deer, Elk, and Moose. Two large kettles, also hanging over the coals from cross-sticks, contain the thick, bubbly substance that we call Berry Soup. Mom once explained to me that the People consider their Berry Soup as a Holy Meal, because their forefathers in the long ago, once, survived a whole Winter on soups made from their dried Berries and Roots, while all the game had left their country for some mysterious reason. She said that the Soup is usually made by boiling water and adding many Service Berries and some cleaned Bitterroots. Pieces of Wild Turnip are put in to thicken the Soup. The roasted meat, the cut-up pieces of vegetables, and the Berry Soup represent all the Holy Food of the People, and makes an especially relishing menu after a Powerful sweat. After our bowls are filled we all take out one berry and hold it aloft, saying our prayers of thanks for the Good Food, the Good Lodges, the Good Gathering, and the Good Life. Then we put the berries down at the edge of the firepit as a spiritual offering to our Mother Earth. Those who are sitting further back pass their berries up to those near the firepit.

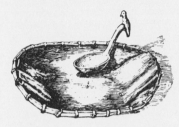

. . . .After eating we all pick up our bowls and any scraps left over, and clean up around ourselves. We will all go home to our lodges to get dressed and comb our hair—to rejoin here later for the singing and dancing. We leave the Lodge looking as it did before we came in. . . . .

I join my own family in walking back to the tipi. We are all elated, filled with food, and excited about the upcoming dance. Father says he is going to take a short nap and I think I will join him. That will give the women a chance to get dressed without us in their way. . . .

. . . .Father awakens me to tell me that the women are already gone to the West Lodge and that the singing there has begun. We both feel a bit foolish for napping so long and must now dress in a hurry so as not to get there too late to be inconspicuous. I get out the rawhide that is folded into a large envelope and contains my fancy dress outfit that the women of the household have been making for me during the past weeks. I take out my new Buckskin leggings, shirt, and aprons and put them on. I've tried the outfit on several times while it was being made, so I know how it goes on and how it fits. It would take me too long to comb and braid my hair, so I'll just brush it well and wear it loose. Father hands me a white Eagle tail feather with a black tip and a tuft of hair.

You should wear this in your hair, he says. *It will represent your great experience of coming to us, here, in this Valley. All of Us, here, know that a single feather in a man's hair means that one event in his Life has been particularly strong for him.* That seems like a most spiritual reason for wearing such a feather, so I gladly tie it to a bunch of hair at the crown of my head. It will sway gently as I move, and its tuft of hair will float in the Air. After I put some garters around my leggings at my ankles, and tie my moccasins, I am ready to go. I'll carry along the beaded sash which was given to me by Two Crows—his great-grandfather had it given to him by the chief of some Eastern tribe as a token of friendship long, long ago. Father is adjusting his Eagle feather headdress. When he sees that I am ready to go he motions me out.

An evening breeze is blowing outside, making the Eagle feather on my head tug at the bunch of hair that it is tied to. The fringes on my shirt and leggings ripple up and down and back and forth as I take each step, while the softness of the Buckskin hides gives me comfortable security and protection from the breeze. The feathers on Father's headdress shimmer in the breeze and rustle quietly—much like the sound made by a gliding Eagle's wings when he sails by with the Wind on a noiseless day. Father is wearing his Buckskin suit, also, and the fringes make his whole body appear to be flowing along. He carries a stick with a single Eagle feather, to remind him of some dramatic experience during his life.

As we approach the West Lodge we can see that the dance has not yet formally begun—since a number of People are still standing around outside. They all have their robes wrapped about their bodies to keep back the chilling evening air. The long fire inside lights up the lodge brightly, and much talking and warm-up singing can be heard. I will stay outside for a few more moments and let Father go in by himself, at first. . . .

Some while later the dance is about to be started. Everyone sits down in the same places as they did for the earlier eating—men on one side, women on the other. Little Bear is handed a filled pipe with which he says a prayer. He then lights the pipe and passes it down the row of men, each one smoking four turns, then passing it on to the next one. The last man passes the pipe back up towards the first man, no one smoking while it goes that way except for young Stone Pipe. As the Keeper of the Sacred Pipe Stem he has inherited the ancient custom of honor by being allowed to smoke from pipes no matter from which direction they are passed to him, as he is spiritually also smoking for the Sacred Stem. The others will only smoke pipes passed to them from their right, in the direction that Sun travels around the circle of the Universe.

While one pipe has been travelling down the row of men, another one has been going down the line of women. Little Bear's woman Fine Sewing lit the pipe for that side and said a prayer with it. The pipe was then passed down to the last woman in the line, who smoked first, so that it could be passed to each smoker in the proper direction.

With the smoking completed Little Bear walks over to the center of the lodge and sits down in front of his large drum, where three of his boys have already seated themselves. A large cup of water is handed to Little Bear, who takes a drink and passes it on to the other boys. The tall one, called Black Eyes drinks a swallow, then takes another mouthful and spurts some of it over his left shoulder, then his right shoulder, then on to the ground between his legs, and the rest into the palms of his hands, which he briskly rubs together. With an almost-coughing tone he makes the sound, *Huh, huh, huh, huh!* Then he rubs his palms over his glossy hair, giving a final and triumphant *Huh!* as he tosses his dangling locks behind his shoulders, shows his white teeth in a big grin, and winks real conspicuously to one of the younger girls seated by her mother in the line of women. Some of the women giggle, and most of the men chuckle from amusement. Meanwhile, Low Horn begins the singing with a drawn-out opening note that is several scales higher than the screaming of most women. Then the drumming begins—rapidly, at first, as the four singers take quick, short strokes with their springy drumsticks. A moments pause in the shrill note and the rapid drumming. . . .then all four begin chanting in a medium-high tone to the loud and steady thumping of the drumsticks.

Father gets up, nodding to two of his friends, Suma and Pemmican and the three slowly begin dancing. Little Bear lays down his drumstick, picks up an Eagle's wing fan, and wraps his Bear robe around him. He joins the other three men, and the four together now circle around the inside of the Lodge in front of the People— they are the honorary dancers who usually lead off in the dancing. All four men dance in a stately fashion—not hopping about like the younger ones will do. They hold their bodies erect and turn their heads from side to side with each step. And their footsteps—their feet move with barely more than a shuffle. Yet, it is a very smooth shuffle that causes each leg to give a slight upward jerk with every drumbeat. Sometimes the men shuffle a bit towards the right, then a bit towards the left, all the while making a smooth and casual circle around the dance ring.

After the honorary dancers have made four circles around the Lodge others begin to get up and start dancing. The dance is just warming up, so no one moves very quickly. Some People stand up and just dance in place, by bouncing their bodies lightly to the beat of the drum, and swaying from side to side. I stand up and join them, and soon the desire for dancing begins to circulate along with my blood. . . .

Little Bear has rejoined his sons in the singing and drumming, and the song is a more lively one. A number of People still remain standing in one place—or dancing within a small area close to their seats. Others are beginning to loosen their bodies a bit—soon they will be involving themselves fully in the ever-increasing tempo and enthusiasm of the drumming and singing. . . .

What a colorful scene is made by the People in their beautiful costumes. Buckskins, furs, feathers, beads, and bells are everywhere. Each one is wearing these things which he or she feels expresses their life with Nature. And each one dances to his own thoughts of the Natural experiences which he has had.

There is old Big Snake, wearing his ancient Buffalo horn headdress. It was given to him long ago by his father Eagle Plume, who made it from the skin and horns of the first Buffalo Bull he ever brought down—years ago, when Buffalo Bulls were still common in the country below. He is blowing on a bone whistle to which are attached the feathers of various Birds that he has dreamed of. His dance imitates the slow, boasting movements of the leading bull in a Buffalo herd. At intervals he blows on his whistle, bends his head low, and prepares a mock charge at one of the other People dancing nearby. Big Snake is a good-natured old man, and everyone is cheered by his antics.

Young Horse Rider is involved in a more lively dance—lifting his knees up high as his feet tap the ground in time to the drumbeats. He turns constantly to the right or left, moving in and out of the dancing group with ease. On his head is a roach made from the hair of a Porcupine, which ripples in the Air from the constant movement. Compared to the measured steps of old Big Snake the rapid movements of Horse Rider make him look like a lively calf running around a serious bull. Yet, both bull and calf seem to be flowing with the same rhythm—dancing to the same tune.

Behind the circle of drummers stands Low Horn's woman, quietly watching the People's involvement with her husband's singing and drumming. The drumsticks bounce far into the air between each beat. As one the sticks come back down to strike the surface of the skin drum another blow, another loud *thump*

which joins the ones before and the ones after to make a rapid steady *Thum, thum, thum, thum,* in rhythm with everyone's heart beat. Low Horn's woman is

holding the sturdy carrier into which their small child is safely strapped. Elaborate bead-work covers its Buckskin bag as well as the Buckskin which is stretched over the long, oval backboard. She often carries the back-board over her shoulders by a strap which is fastened to its backside. The white background of the beadwork contrasts brightly with the yellow-brown color of the smoked Buckskin from which her dress is made. The top of the dress is covered with numerous teeth from Elk which Low Horn has brought home for their meals—each tooth represents a hunting experience and a lot of good meals.

Whenever the drummers and singers take a break some-one gets up before the group to tell some brief, old-time story, or to explain about some new article of dress that is being worn for the first time tonight, or to sing some song for the enter-tainment of the People. The others take seats around the floor, or step outside for some cool air or a short walk.

At intervals between the fast and energetic dance numbers come the slower Owl Dance tunes. They are recognizable by their hard-soft, beats and by the reaction among the People. These are the dances where men and women join together in couples—arms around each others' waists—as they dance sideways in a circle around the lodge. As each Owl Dance progresses, the various couples join others, until a long, Snake-like line forms and coils its way back and forth around the lodge. The dancers move to the left, picking up their left feet first and stomping them down in time to the loud beat. With the soft beat they drag their right feet behind, thus taking short steps while their bodies rise and fall with each beat. When all the People have joined in one line those at the front weave around so that they are dancing past those at the rear. Often the Snake is so coiled around the dance floor that all one can see is many smiling faces, bouncing bodies, and tapping footsteps, going to and fro.

Songbird's voice has awakened us early, again. Father and I have just returned from a plunge into the lake to help awaken our bodies. I am rubbing myself dry with the help of my robe. Outside, I can hear the distant splashing of water at the lake, as others awaken themselves likewise. Sun is just about to show His Power over the mountain tops—already His streams of light are making bright the early-morning blue Sky.

Today and tomorrow—the second and third days of the Summer's End Ceremony—we will all be going to the gardens to bring in the Season's harvests. During the afternoons and evenings we will have more drumming and singing— and we will continue to dance. First, we will all be meeting at the Sacred Tobacco Garden. . . .

. . . .The Tobacco plants have been growing all Summer in a small plot of land which juts out into a quiet, tiny bay of the lake near the camp. The soil there is continually damp from the surrounding waters, while Sun's rays are able to reach the plants all day long. Yet, the spot is so protected by low, surrounding bluffs that the strong breezes which regularly blow across the lake pass right over the top of the plants without causing them any harm.

The garden is divided up into numerous small plots—each one belonging to one of the camp's families. Each plot has a spiritual guardian—represented physically by one or more tiny dolls made from Buckskin and hair. The little dolls are attached to long, carved sticks which are planted in the ground at the head of each plot. Bells and chimes made of shells and beads are attached to other sticks planted around the plots, and little colored pieces of cloth and ribbon wave gaily in the air. At first glance the scene looks like a carnival for little People held in a forest of towering, green plants, with banners waving and musical notes coming from the different things hanging on sticks.

Only the upper parts of the People are visible as they wander among the Sacred Plants in the garden—each family coming together at the head of their own plot. Everyone present plucks a leaf from one of the Plants and holds it aloft, towards the warm-shining Sun. Someone begins to pray and then we all join in—each one giving thanks for the goodness of the past Summer and for the wealth of the Sacred Tobacco crop. When we finish praying we put our leaves into the soil around the carved sticks with the guardians attached—a symbolic sharing of the crop with its spiritual guardians. Then everyone begins to pull up the plants to the tune of a song that is started by Songbird. The words say:

Sun, Above is Holy.   Earth, Below is Holy.   These Sacred Plants are Holy.
Our smoking will be Holy.   Our lives will be Powerful.

The plants are pulled up firmly and carefully, so that the roots will remain attached. The soil is then carefully shaken from the roots and the plant is placed in a pile. It is saddening to watch the disappearance of that beautiful garden of swaying, living green. But it is pleasant to think of the many spiritual gatherings and ceremonies which will be started by the sacred smoking of these plants.

Mother has explained to me what we will do with the plants when we get them back home. The roots will be cut off and washed. They keep well and will be used to season our Winter's cooking. The seeds will then be carefully picked and placed in special Buckskin pouches—to be saved for later plantings. Father told me that some years the plants grow too slowly to give mature seeds, so that the People must always be very careful with their seed gathering and try to keep enough to last for several years. The rest of the plant is then hung upside down from the ceiling of the lodge until it becomes dry and brittle. The leaves are then carefully removed and ground up inside of large pouches, where they will be kept until needed for smoking. The stems are cut up into small pieces and mixed with the leaves of the Bearberry plant to be used for just everyday smoking. Sometimes the stems are put in with fried foods to be used for seasoning, though they are too tough and bitter to be eaten.

After all the plants have been pulled up—even the little ones that have spent most of the Summer hidden in the shade of the tall plants—the head of each household brings out the family's Eagle plume offering to the Spirits who are at the Sacred Garden all year. One of Little Bear's sons is selected to take all the plumes down to the shore of the lake and place them in the ground in a row.

Before the Winter snows come the men will return to the Garden with loads of manure, which they will give to the Earth in exchange for what they have taken today. Then they will each take up their Eagle plume offering and plant it in the center of their family plot. Every year the People have taken their Sacred Tobacco harvest this way—and every year they have had a successful crop.

With a Powerful feeling of one-ness we return to our lodges, everyone's arms filled with huge bunches of plants, their whispy roots dangling down towards their Mother Earth for the last time—their bright green leaves swaying in the breeze once more, before they will be turning into smoke and joining the breezes forever, at later times.

. . . .Tonight we dance, again. The dance is to start outside of the big Earth Lodge before the coming of evening.

Little Bear will lead the singing—the drumming will be done on the Turtle drums that were made by Suma during one of his visits to the mountains. They are made of the thick part of a Moose hide—taken from behind the neck. They were cut out in the shape of the Turtles that Suma saw in his dream, and then sewn up while still wet. Sand was stuffed inside of them so that they would keep their shape until dry. Little Bear's sons will be taking turns standing before the entryway to the Earth lodge and giving prayers of thanks while holding the smoking pipe. While praying, Little Bear told me, they will be thinking of the many good songs and dances that the People have enjoyed during the past year, and they will be asking for another year of such goodness. Later on, as darkness comes, the singers will move inside the Earth lodge, where we will all gather for our evening meal and for more Owl dancing. . . .

. . . .Tomorrow we are to harvest the fruit from the trees and the vegetable from the garden—it has been a very successful Season and we will have a large harvest. Much of the crop will be dried for Winter use. Some of it will be stored in the underground cellar, where it will keep as it is. Some of it will have to be eaten within a short time after the ending of the days-long Ceremony. The harvest will be prepared during the four days of the Sun Dance, by those who are not taking a direct part in that ceremony. The preparing will be done around the sacred shelter lodge inside of which the Sun Dance itself will be going on. I have not yet been told much about the Sun Dance Ceremony, except  that it will begin on the day after Stone Pipe opens his Bundle and brings out the Sacred Pipe.

This is the fourth day of the Summer's End Ceremony—the day that Stone Pipe is to open his Bundle and take out the Sacred Pipe Stem, so that we can all give prayers of thanks for the good Summer, and the plentiful harvest, and that we can all encourage each other to look forward to a good Winter.

All night long Stone Pipe's voice has been drifting across the bay into the camp. He has been praying and singing while he is on top of the rock cliff that faces the camp from across the water. He will soon begin his walk back to camp to lead in the Holy Ceremony. Two Crows has been preparing the double lodge in which the ceremony will be held. The double lodge is made from two sets of lodge poles built up in such a way as to take two regular lodge covers—thus forming one oblong lodge that is large enough to seat everyone comfortably while still having enough room for the sacred dancing which will be a part of it. Mother is just giving me some of her robes to take over to the big lodge to use for making couches for the People. I will take them over and help Two Crows with his duties. . . .

. . . .Some time has already passed since Songbird went around the camp playing Stone Pipe's sacred flute and calling out to the People to assemble in the double lodge. Everyone has come in and taken a seat among one of the two rows of People. In the center, at the West end of the lodge, sits Stone Pipe. Songbird sits at his left and the Sacred Bundle rests on a pile of furs between them. Stone Pipe has been telling us the story of the Dreams which have been directing him in assembling the Sacred Bundle, and he is just now telling about the Sacred Pipe Stem that is kept within it:

. . . .So my father followed the instructions of his Dream and went into the Mountains to hide the Sacred Pipe Stem in a cave. He hiked for four days before he reached the top of Chief Mountain, fasting the whole time. He carried the Pipe Stem tied across his back, and brought with him only a blanket, his knife, and a sack of Pemmican to eat on the way home. Several times he encountered Grizzly Bears on the trails along the high, barren slopes of the mountains. Each time he took the Pipe stem from his back and held the Bundle out to give the Bears a smoke, singing one of the Pipe's ancient Power Songs. Always the Bears let him pass without harm.

Just below the flat top of Chief Mountain my father found the cave—and just then the Winds, which had been increasing, began carrying drops of rain which quickly turned into a torrent. My father found safety inside the cave and looked out at the Lightning ceremony which was taking place in the gray and black Sky. He was exhausted and quickly became overpowered—His Spirit left his body there and travelled on a fabulous journey. He travelled ahead in Life and saw scenes which were not to occur for many years, yet.

The first thing he saw was the approach of countless People coming Westward across the Plains. The People were similar to the ones that had, by that time, already been building cabins and towns here and there in our Old Country. But they were thousands of times more numerous—swarming like flies over the Land so that the Land was barely visible any longer. In between these hordes of People my father was able to get glimpses of the Land, and it looked frightening—the many feet and hooves and wheel had broken down the bushes, scraped all the trees, smashed all the grasses, and left muddy ruts and tears in our Earth Mother's skin that he could hardly bear to see. He saw what happened to the camps of our People—they were knocked over and the pieces were scattered all over—only those People survived who joined the masses and moved along with them. Here and there a handful of others were saved—usually those who were off on some sidehill or up some mountain seeking visions or otherwise involved in Holy Thoughts.

My father was shown that the Spirit of the Old People would be lost unless some of it was taken up into the mountains—to some remote area where it would be safe. Our own valley, here, was the one he saw as the safe place for the Spirit to remain. He saw the closing of the mountain pass—our only gate—which he correctly predicted for the People before it happened. He saw our People living in Harmony with Nature, here. And he foresaw that someday the thoughtless mass of new People would begin to think again. He foresaw that the Spirit of the Old People would come back to Life someday in the Persons of the Young People, everywhere. He said that when that Spirit was to be reborn, and not until then, would we, as the Keepers of that Spirit's living Powers, again come in contact with People outside of our Hidden Valley in the Mountains. He said "a tiny hole will burst in the dam of this Sacred Reservoir of our Spirit—a tiny hole in the form of a Person. And that Person shall be carrying the Spirit of Me and shall have the Power to distribute All the Power which has guided our Old People through their lives. And when that Person comes," my father said, "he shall dance the Sun Dance with you and during those four days I will let him know who I am, what Power I have to give him, and how he will have to pass that Power on to the many who will come after him from his part of the World, seeking It." That is what my father said, my relatives, and that is the reason why this Summer's End Ceremony will be the most Holy and Powerful of All the ones we have had, for the time has come for Our Power to go forth and bring Happiness throughout the Land, wherever it is needed. The tiny hole has burst and our reservoir is now connected with the outside World!

The howling of a Wolf somewhere across the lake brings the startling reality of Natural Life back to everyone's Minds—not a sound has been made since Stone Pipe finished speaking. Now Stone Pipe looks up with a smile and says:

My father's sacred guardian was the Wolf—whenever he was in need for the Wolf's power he gave the Wolf's howl. His Spirit is with us now.

I suddenly have an immense feeling of insignificance—my own thoughts seem petty and small. At the same time I feel as though the Earth is balanced on my head and my arms could stretch out endlessly across the Universe. What Power there is in existence to cause all of this to happen. As nothing is the human body, with its limitations, when compared with the limitless expanse that makes up the realm of the Mind. Perhaps just a minor test to see if our Universal Minds can escape the confinements of our Earthly bodies.

From two large, skin sacks behind him Stone Pipe brings out several handfuls of rawhide rattles of the kind that I once saw him make. He sews together two pieces of wet rawhide cut out with necks for handles. Through the necks he pours sand and pounds it down with a short stick until the main part of the rattle looks like a round bulb. After the rawhide dries in that shape he pours the sand back out, inserts a few pebbles, and puts the stick inside the neck to make a stronger handle. Each of the rattles is covered with Sacred Red paint. He passes the rattles around until most everyone has one. He also brings out some bunches of dried and cleaned Animal hooves, fastened to long buckskin thongs which are tied together at one end. They are used as rattles, also, and their jingling sounds can be heard while they are being passed from hand to hand among the People.

. . . .And now we are all singing the Holy Songs in time to the beating of the rattles—Stone Pipe and Songbird are leading each song. Dozens of rattles at once: *chk*, *chk*, *chk*, *chk*, in harmony. Dozens of voices chanting the tunes that we have often sang together in the past, while Stone Pipe and Songbird add the words about the holiness of our thoughts, our lives, and our Spirits. After the fourth song Stone Pipe lays down his rattle and turns towards the Sacred Bundle, though he continues to sing with the rest of us. This is the song that we always sing when sweat bathing, but Stone Pipe adds some words to it this time:

You stand up, you take me, you untie me, I am Powerful;
You stand up, you take me, you untie me, I am Strong!

He sings the words as though they were coming from the Bundle to him, while he reaches towards the knot at the end of the Bundle's buckskin thong. Once he reaches for it. . . .twice he reaches. . . .three times. . . .and the fourth time he takes a hold of it and gives it a quick jerk which brings the knot loose. He unwinds the long thongs and stands up with just the Sacred Pipe Stem Bundle in his hands—the skin of a Wolf wrapped about it so that it cannot be seen.

Songbird, meanwhile, has taken a glowing coal from the fireplace with his Sacred Tongs made from the forked branch of a berry bush. He sprinkles some of the Sweet Pine needles on the coal, while the song still goes on. For a moment the smoke from the needles wavers just above them, then it spirals hurriedly up into the air and passes throughout the lodge, the wonderful sweet scent brings happiness into our bodies and good thoughts into our minds. Everyone grasps a handful of the Holy Smell and brings it to his heart to signify the becoming of one with the goodness and the heart.

Stone Pipe passes the Sacred Pipe over the smoke four times, and is now getting back down on his knees to bring the Holy Stem out from its wrappings of skin and fine, ancient cloths. Meanwhile, he sings the words:

> Man, you must say it, my Pipe it is Powerful;
>
> Man, you must say it, my Pipe it is Strong!

He lifts the Sacred Stem from its last covering and holds it up in the Air for All to behold. Its covering of countless, white Eagle plumes ripples in the vibrations of the Air within the lodge, caused by the Power of our singing and rattling. As smiles of recognition and happiness cover the singing faces, hands reach into the air towards the Pipe and are brought back to rest on breasts. The People take the Power represented by the Pipe into their hearts. Stone Pipe begins a new song, which everyone quickly takes up. He sings the words:

> There comes the Old Man, he is coming walking;
> He Ja Ha, He Ja Ha, He Ja He Ja Hey.
> He's coming in here, sitting down, that Old Man is Powerful!
> He Ja Ha, He Ja Ha, He Ja He Ja Hey.

During this song he dances slowly, with smooth, jerking steps, to the Four Directions, beginning with the East, where Sun rises. At each place he holds the Sacred Stem at arm's length, offering a smoke to the Spirit of that direction by aiming the mouthpiece that way. Next, he dances to the North, where the North Star shines brightly from one place, and where the Powers of Winters dwell. As he dances to the West the words of the song change and tell about the Old Woman, who is coming in to be with the Old Man Spirit, and Us. To the West is Sun's nighttime home, where the other half of the World begins. Finally, he dances toward the South, from where come the warm winds of Summer that help to make everything grow.

After Stone Pipe sits back down with the Sacred Pipe he begins another song, this one with the words:

Old Man he says, "let us smoke," It is Powerful!

He turns the Pipe all the way around once, holding the mouthpiece towards each one of us as it goes around. Then he sings:

Old Man, he says, "my old smoke, I do not feel it."

At this he shakes the Stem four times, so that the Eagle plumes dangling from it sway wildly in the air. The chant continues, and Stone Pipe now sings:

Old Man, he says, "my new smoke, I feel it." It is Powerful!

As the rattling continues with a steady beat and a number of People go on chanting softly, Stone Pipe holds the Sacred Stem close to his head and begins to pray aloud:

HiYo Sacred Stem—All of You Powerful Spirits who are here with us! We thank You for letting us be here all together again, at the end of another good Summer. We are thankful for our good health—our good food—our good homes—our Sacred Valley Home. We ask you to show us always your Powers, Sacred Pipe. Show us your Powers so that we will be inspired to live Holy and that we will have the strength to live well. Give us strength by letting us know that you are always with us—All of you Powers of the Universe—All of you who are Holy. . . .

Stone Pipe asks for continued strength and happiness and talks about the times to come, before the next Summer's End Ceremony in Four Seasons. Then he passes the Pipe to his left, where my father is sitting. Father accepts the Pipe Stem with both hands and, beginning at the top of his head, rubs the Sacred Stem down along each side of his body twice while praying aloud and asking the Powers to be fully with him and help him to keep away from any evil. After he finishes his prayer he, too, passes the Pipe to his left, and so it continues around the lodge, each one saying a prayer loudly or silently and spending some intimate moments with the Ancient Holy Thing.

After the Sacred Pipe has gone all around, Stone Pipe takes it again and stands at the back of the lodge with it—holding it aloft again so that all may see it. My father removes his robe and his shirt and kneels down behind the ancient Buffalo skull in front of the altar. He takes the smoking pipe from the place where it is resting on a frame of willow sticks—mouthpiece toward the Sky so that All the Spirits may feel invited to smoke. He holds the pipe up and calls out:

Great Power of everything! Smoke with us now, as we take the first taste of our Holy Smoking Crop of this Season. Be with us through the coming Seasons and give us good thoughts even when times are hard. Let the glowing warmth of this smoking mixture represent the warmth we will have this Winter. Let the greenness of the unburnt leaves represent the good food we will then be eating. Let this stone bowl represent the strength of our bodies. Let this pipe stem represent the straightness of our lives.

So, now the smoking pipe makes its way around the lodge, passing from Person to Person—each one taking four slow whisps of the Holy Smoke. When the pipe returns to the rear of the lodge father refills it and puts it back in its place against the willow support. Stone Pipe walks forward and places the Holy Pipe Stem against the willow support, next to the smoking pipe. He goes back to his place by the rest of the Bundle and sits down. From behind the Bundle he brings forth his long flute, licks his lips, and puts his mouth against the mouthpiece—exhaling softly to cause the flute to exclaim a quiet and pretty note. The musical sound flows through the lodge like an unseen cloud of smoke, joining us all together in its tonal sea of beauty. We all close our eyes, as Stone Pipe asked us to do earlier, and bring to Mind the dreams which he told us about. The Thoughts evoke visual scenes of his serenades for the many Birds and Animals with which he visits in his dreams. We All know well the ways of those Birds and Animals, so it is easy to see them now, walking alongside of young Stone Pipe who is playing his Sacred Flute. . . .For some time he plays his Sacred Flute, while I sway my body to the rhythms of his tunes. Some are humming along with the tunes—causing a vibration which makes the music become more than sound, as it goes into my ears and throughout my body and Mind.

The sound of Stone Pipe's Sacred Flute begins to grow dim, but the humming, swaying, and vibrations continue. Stone Pipe makes gentle grunting and growling noises, and I barely open my eyes to watch him lifting up the skin of a Black Bear and swaying back and forth with it, while squatting on his haunches. He sings a song, in rhythm to our humming, and calls out the words:

In Summer I eat Berries; in Winter I stay warm and sleep. My Life is good. My Life is Powerful.

He hands the Bear skin to father, on his left, who immediately covers his head with it and quietly begins chanting a song-prayer. Stone Pipe, meanwhile, brings out a Bird skin from his Bundle—the skin of a Loon. He holds the body of the Bird in his left arm—cradled like a baby—and with his right hand he holds the head up in such a way that the Loon seems to be swimming. He moves his arms back and forth and sways with his body and sings these words:

I live where there is water. Water is my Medicine. My water life is good. My water life is Powerful.

With my eyes still barely open I can hardly see Stone Pipe. But I can see the firelight reflecting brightly from the Loons shiny feathers, while the flickering shadows on the lodge walls begin to look like the continual movement of the water at the edge of a river. I see the Loon swimming back and forth in that water—I begin to feel as though I, too, were swimming along with that Loon in the water.

Father has, meanwhile, passed the Bear skin down the line, to his left. Stone Pipe now gives him the Loon skin, which he also cradles in his arms and sways with in time to his chanting.

Stone Pipe reaches into the Bundle and brings out the shiny, brown skin of a Beaver—the paddle-like tail hanging from the almost-round body. He hangs the skin over his right arm and grasps the tail with his left hand. He slaps the tail on his back and sings the words:

My food is on the Land, but my home is safely in the Water. My Earth Life is good. My water life is Powerful.

Like the Loon, the Beaver seems to come alive as Stone Pipe moves it back and forth as if it were swimming—now dipping its head down into the Bundle and bringing back a short stick whose ends have been noticeably Beaver chewed. The Beaver makes the motions of building himself a home, and I begin to feel as though I, too, were carrying sticks with me to help him with the building of his home. . . .

. . . . Stone Pipe continues to bring out the skins of other Birds and Animals—for each one he makes the gestures which seem to bring it to life. For each one he sings the song of its Life Power. The Duck's song says:

I fly in the Air. I fly where my food is. Air is my Medicine. My life in Air is Powerful.

The song of the Grouse says:

I make my home in the bushes of the forest. That is where I drum and dance. The forest is my Medicine. My forest life is Powerful.

By this time everyone in the lodge has some Bird or Animal skin and is either humming or praying while swaying with it. Some of the People are making the sounds of the different Animals, and it feels as though All of Nature were taking part in this ceremony of Life. Many Spirits are flowing about and being interchanged from one to another. The feeling is very Powerful. . . .

. . . .There will be four of us dancing during the four holy days and nights of the Sun Dance Ceremony. Songbird will be guiding us and Singing in the Night will sit in her sacred booth and fast along with us. After Stone Pipe completed the ceremony with his Sacred Bundle, last night, Songbird asked me if I understood, now, that I was to take part in the Powerful Sun Dance Experience. He told me to eat lightly of the tasty Berry Soup that was served after the ceremony, and to prepare my self spiritually for eating nothing at all during the next four days. I had been planning to eat nothing but light portions of Berry Soup during that time, as everyone else in camp is doing, but I had not planned on going without food altogether. Yet, I know that everyone in the camp will be praying for me and anxiously awaiting my meeting with my Guardian Spirit—Stone Pipe's long-gone father. I could only hope to accomplish that meeting by going without food, as was required by the Ancients in the long ago. So, I knew that I could endure the fast.

It is not yet light outside, but already the camp is astir. Old Songbird will be taking us four holy dancers up on the cliff to await the coming of Sun. The Sky is clear outside and it promises to give us a fine day.

I am to wear only my breechclout and a pair of moccasins and a large fur robe to keep warm my body. As I step outside I see Songbird waiting at the

place of the Holy Lodge. It is still fairly dark, but I can see that he, too, is wearing a large fur robe around his body. On his feet are a pair of beautifully-beaded moccasins, and in one hand he carries a large fan made from the wing of an Eagle. His hair is hanging down in loose folds. And perched on top of his head—tied to his hair—is the body of his Guardian Power—a powerful Eagle. Songbird stands silently. The air about him seems more sacred than ever.

I walk over and stand near Songbird, neither of us saying a word in the cool darkness. Stone Pipe joins us a moment later, dressed in robe and moccasins like myself. In a few more moments the other two holy dancers join us from out of the dark—Savaro and Little Bear's son Low Horn. Songbird turns and quietly walks towards the shore of the lake—the four of us following noiselessly.

. . . .After walking all the way around the edge of the bay and then passing through the forest trail, we are now climbing up the last slope to reach the top of the cliff which overhangs the lakeshore. Countless persons have come here to seek visions or just meditate and sing Power Songs in private.

. . . .Three times Songbird calls for the boys outside to lift the door flap—but we don't go outside. The fourth time he pours the remaining water on the stones and tells us to rush into the cold lake water to rinse off. A scramble follows, after which the only sound is the breaking of water as four bodies dive into the deep pool which lies just beyond the sweat lodge. . . .I feel much like a hot ember just taken from a fire and dropped into a vessel of water. . . .the coldness only tingles my skin, but does not enter my body. Quickly I return to the surface and swim to shore. Songbird is standing in the shallow water, rubbing handfuls of it over his body. He is afraid that a sudden plunge into the cold water might be too strong an experience for his aging body, so he rinses off more casually. In just a few moments we all have our moccasins and breechclouts on again as we follow Songbird over and into the Holy Lodge.

Songbird has us sit down in front of the Center Pole, which seems to be supporting the whole lodge as the hub of a spoked wheel. Its top points toward the endless heights of the Sky, while its base is wrapped with seed necklaces and strings of dried berries which the People tied there as symbolic offerings to the Universal Spirits, with good thoughts of having much more of these good things. A dozen steps beyond the Center Pole, in the direction which we are facing, is the Pine bough arbor in which sits Singing In the Night—the spiritual representative for the women. She sits with her head bowed, her unbraided hair hanging loosely over her robe.

Your sacrifice of dancing before this Center Pole for the People, while not eating for the whole time, will give inspiration to All and life-long Powerful thoughts to yourselves, says Songbird, while looking at each of us with his pleasant eyes. *This Pole before you is Your Center of the Universe—Everything radiates from here in equally never—ending paths. All those paths converge right here, and You may choose to walk down any of them that You wish. You must only WISH. During your days and nights here, if anything inspires You along these paths that you will visit, share your inspirations with Us. We will be All Together, here, to give strength to each other.*

Songbird walks over to the arbor and helps Singing In the Night to get up. He lays his robe inside the arbor and picks up his Buckskin pipe bag, which is laying in there. Then the two come and sit before us.

Let Your thoughts dwell often on the Power of our being here, says Songbird, *so that your sacrifice will express your gratitude for that Power. Life here, on Earth, would be of no use if it gave us nothing to be grateful for. Be happy that you are here, All of You, and You will have more than enough to be grateful for!*

Songbird has filled his pipe and he now rests the stem against the Center Pole, sitting the bowl carefully on the ground beneath it. He rises up and, again, assists Singing In the Night to do so.

Dawn has already made its appearance by the time we finally reach the little clearing at the top of the cliff. Songbird still says nothing—he only turns toward the East and stands in silence. We stand behind him and wait for the golden glow with him.

. . . .Not long—and the Eastern horizon begins its daily, spectacular color show. First orange, then red, then pink, and then orange again, as that ever-present Spirit of Sun comes into view over the mountains.

HiYo Sun—you bringer of warmth and brightness, calls out Songbird in a loud, clear voice. *HiYo Sun—You who are the center of our Universe, so vast that we cannot begin to imagine All the Power. Pity Us—we here, on this Earth. We, who are so small and insignificant compared to All that there is. Guide Us to live in harmony with All of the Spirits of the Universe. Make our Paths bright so that we may see the way to goodness. Make our hearts warm so that we will give each time that we take. Shine down on Us, Holy Sun, during each one of these next four days, and be with Us completely while we give up our thoughts to the Power of You. And let that Power remain with us during the coming Seasons.*

With his prayer finished Songbird turns and begins walking down the path towards camp. Silently, the rest of us follow him—down from that high cliff to the shore of the water that can be seen far below. The rocky trail zig-zags back and forth before entering the forest, where it becomes a dirt trail with a more gradual grade. Sun's light filters through the trees and gives the forest and clearings a contrasting appearance of dark and bright. The coolness of the morning forest is already broken in those places where Sun has had a chance to enter. It will be a very warm end-of-Summer day.

Back at the camp the People have already finished covering the framework of the Holy Lodge. Pine boughs have been laid over the roof poles, which radiate outward from the tall center pole—the pole which stands in the middle of the lodge. At their outer points the roof poles are fastened to upright posts, which are attached to other cross-poles, the whole forming a round structure similar to the main camp hall, but without any siding, roofing, or floor, other than the numerous Pine boughs.

Songbird leads the way to the sweat lodge at the edge of camp, down by the lakeshore. Several young boys are there tending the fire which is heating the rocks. The coverings are already on the lodge, so we crawl through the door-way and sit down around the inside—Songbird sitting at the rear. Unlike the spacious camp sweat lodge this one has barely enough room for the four of us and our leader. We pass our robes outside—and the boys begin pushing red-hot stones in through the doorway with forked sticks. Eight stones is all that Song-bird wants them to pass in—eight stones, each the size of a fist. Songbird sings the Sweat Bath Song as he begins to sprinkle water on the hot rocks. . . .

We will have a Holy Smoke after Singing In the Night purifies her body in the sweat lodge, says **Songbird,** *then we will begin with our dancing.*

The four of us sit quietly while Songbird and Singing In the Night walk down to the lakeshore. There is silence in the camp—all the People are in their lodges awaiting the start of the dancing. Voices can barely be heard, talking in low tones. Only Birds continue to talk about daily life, while flying through the Air and hopping about, unseen, in the many trees around the camp.

After some time comes the distant sound of breaking water—telling us that Singing In the Night has completed her sweat bath. . . .In a while she comes back into the Holy Lodge enclosure with Songbird. She is wearing her robe about her body, her loose hair hanging over it in dark, wet locks.

After we are all seated together again, here in front of the Center Pole, Songbird picks up his pipe and holds it aloft, asking the Spirits everywhere to smoke with us and give us good thoughts. He lights it and puffs briefly, then passes the pipe to Singing In the Night, who does the same. The pipe makes several rounds before it is smoked out—all of us remaining still and silent during the smoking.

To give our Minds and bodies further Power, during these holy times, **Songbird** tells us, *we will paint ourselves with the Sacred Earth Paint.* He reaches into his pipe bag and brings out a rolled up little sack. The sack contains a quantity of the powder-like red Earth which is found up on the side of one of the mountains, and which the People use at times for painting their faces or covering their holy things.

Songbird reaches into the powdered Earth and brings out a piece of fat, which he begins rubbing between his palms as he gets up on his knees and starts the painting song. The words are:

Sacred Paint—I am looking for it.

He puts the piece of fat back in with the paint and presses one of his greasy, red palms upon his forehead—leaving a bright red imprint which looks like the rising of Sun in the morning. He sings the second song, which says:

Sacred Paint—I have found it. It is Powerful.

At that he wipes his hands all over his face, his hair, his neck, and his arms. Then he turns to Singing In the Night and does the same, singing the second song as he begins painting. He does the same to each of us, in turn, each time singing the second song. After all our faces are covered with the shiny coat of Sacred Paint Songbird removes his robe and motions for us to do the same. He passes the paint-coated piece of fat around so that each of us can rub it well between the palms of our hands, then he motions for us to follow him in rubbing the paint all over our bodies. All the while he continues to chant the second song, without singing the words. When we finish, Singing In the Night puts her robe back on—the rest of us stand up and get ready to begin the dancing. Singing In the Night returns to the arbor and sits back down, hanging her head in prayer. From a rawhide case next to her she takes out an object of upright feathers and hanging skins and beads. She places it on her head. It is the Sacred Headdress which she inherited from the Old Lady who adopted her while still a baby. The headdress has been worn by countless Holy Women in the past, during their People's Summer Ceremonies. Its presence is a constant reminder to Singing In the Night of the example she should make of her Holy Life.

Songbird goes to the arbor and brings out his hand drum—its hide covering stretched tightly across its round, wooden frame from the heat of Sun. On the cover is painted a large red circle, to represent the Power of Sun, and many small, white circles, to represent the Powers of Hail and Thunder. He turns and faces the Center Pole—and Us—and holds the drum up towards the Sky with his left hand. In his right hand he has a slender stick with Buckskin wrapped around its end. Very slowly he lifts his right arm up to bring the drumstick close to the drum—raising his wrinkled face upwards at the same time. His eyes are closed and both of his arms are trembling from excitement and old age.

WHUMM! is the sound that echoes from inside the handdrum out to our eardrums—and all around the camp, as Songbird gives the face of the drum a swift tap with the stick. I look Skyward to peer into the depths of the brilliant blue which surrounds all the Earth.

WHUMM! goes the drum again, with a sharp, penetrating sound that makes my body start as though it had been hit by the drumstick.

WHUMM! goes the drum for a third time, and *WHUMM!* again for a fourth time. At the last beat comes a high, shrill scream from within the arbor that can only be the voice of a woman. It is a musical scream—a song from deep within the lungs of Singing In the Night. It tapers off in a tremolo caused by a rapid flicking of the tongue against the upper roof of the mouth—the moving, crying song of a Holy Woman in rhapsody. For a moment there is silence in the camp—even the Birds in the Air and trees have paused to listen to the echoes in the mountains of Singing In the Night's voice which has been carried far and wide by that one deep breath of Universal Power. . . .

. . . .The cry seems to echo and re-echo countless times from canyons and mountain walls around Us and above Us. At last it echoes no more, and Songbird brings his arm down, though leaving his face up towards the Sky, and begins a steady *Whumm, Whumm, Whumm, Whumm* beat on his drum, while Singing In the Night begins singing a most haunting tune of long, drawn-out vocables.

Haaaaaaiiiiiiiii-Jaaaaaaaaaaaah. . . .*Waaaaaaaaayyyyyyyyyy-Yoooooooooooo-ooooaahh.* . . .her voice floats away with the drum beats. The voices of other women around the camp now join her voice to make a chorus, singing a vibrant mountain song.

After a brief pause in the singing—while only the steady drum beats go on—Singing In the Night begins the song again, joined by the women and then the men, some singing with deep voices and some with the high shrill ones of younger age. The other voices are growing louder and coming closer together as the People of the camp come out from their lodges and walk slowly to the Holy Lodge. . . .

Around the inside of the Holy Lodge the People march, slowly, while the singing and drumming continues—the procession of the Gathering in the Holy Lodge. Only after All the People have come inside and circled the Center Pole several times does the singing stop. The People spread their robes on the ground and sit down upon them. There is silence, again.

Songbird breaks the silence by calling aloud for All to Hear:

We are thankful, Spirits of the Universe, for Being! We are thankful for Being during these past Seasons, and ask All of you Powers to continue to Let It Be! Continue to give Us the strength to endure, to find Happiness in All and Everything, to lead a Holy Life, and to be who we are. . .These next four days that we will spend fully with You, Powers of the Universe; let them be Holy Days. Show Us that You are with us—give Us Your continued inspiration and guidance. Let It Be. . . .Let It Be Good!

Everyone, here, repeats, *Let It Be Good, Let It Be Good*, then everyone begins praying loudly—putting into words the Good Thoughts which are theirs right now for being here together, in good health.

After the last Person has finished praying, Songbird speaks again:

My People, let Us All be happy and strong together, as we have been in the Past. Let this celebration give Us All the Power to go on living this Holy Life during the coming Seasons—the Power to accept those things directed by Nature and to see Everything as being a part of the goodness which Is the Great Power of the Universe.

And so begins the drumming again. Others have brought hand drums, like Songbird's, and are now joining with him to keep the spiritual rhythm going. The songs, too, are sung by many voices, while my eyes are still deep in the blue which colors the vastness Above. . . .

. . . .Much later—I lay down upon my robe which is spread behind me on the ground. I still keep my eyes on the vastness Above, where many more Spirits are beginning to make their appearance in the forms of Stars. The drumming and singing has been going on continually all afternoon. . . .Going on continually all night. . . .going on continually all the next morning. . . .the next afternoon. . . . the next night. . . .

. . . .Dancing—dancing—dancing—looking upward, forever upward. To where? Endlessly—endlessly, as the Universe goes on to a Forever that will take Us forever to experience. . . .giving me a feeling of great insignificance—a grain of sand in the ocean. . . .giving me a feeling of great Power—to be continually surrounded by so much, that there is no way to come to an end, even if this insignificant, Earthly body of mine ceased right now to function. . . . .I lay on my robe—feeling as though my body actually IS ceasing to function—only a numbness left, physically, while my Mind traverses the Universe with great, leaping bounds—looking back down at the tiny ball that is Earth—unable to even see this Hidden Valley, much less my body. . . .Now back to Earth and my body again—hearing the call of the drumming and singing—feeling the need of the others in the Holy Lodge for my presence to be there. . . .

. . . .I sit up and look around in the Star-lit darkness—feeling that others are there, but seeing nothing. The drumming and singing seems very distant—like the echoes in the mountains. A faint orange glow shows at the top of the mountains—I think it is in the direction where Sun sets each evening—it is a faint orange glow that looks like liquid, softly undulating as if being stirred by some distant breeze. . . .undulating at the top of the mountains, as if balanced there and making an effort not to flow over. . . .now it seems so far away—again it seems to come so close that I can reach out and dive my hands into it. . . .I reach both of my hands out for it—closer. . . .and closer. . . .and closer it comes, turning brighter orange as it comes near. . . .and a breeze comes with it—the breeze that is causing the undulating, for the breeze and the movement of the orange has a harmonious rhythm. . . .a warm breeze, it is—warm and whistling, it rustles through the Pine boughs that surround me—I can hear them swishing together and flapping against the poles to which they are fastened. . . .stronger it grows—the rushing of that breeze—stronger as the orange glow becomes brighter and continues to come nearer. . . .and still there is drumming and singing around me—somewhere, near or far; I can't tell just where it's coming from. . . .the breeze has now turned into a full Wind, which sounds like a mountain stream as it rushes through the trees of the forest nearby—sounds, like a hundred People whistling and brushing against each other as it passes through the Holy Lodge and causes the pole foundation to creak and sway. . . .

. . . .The singing and the drumming, the howling of the Wind all around—they seem to be as one, the song is carried by the Wind as though it were coming from the orange glow that now seems to be balanced on top of the Center Pole—an orange glow with no real form and no dimensions. . . .I lean forward—my arms and hands still outstretched—and grasp the Center Pole to steady myself while looking, still, upward. The Pole is warm—very warm—and it is vibrating to the singing. . . .somewhere there is a voice—I can barely hear it—talking, or singing-talking—it is hard to tell which. . . .a voice unlike any I have ever heard before—and it seems to be coming down from Above, down from the top of the Center Pole where the orange glow is still resting and hovering. . . .

Do You feel this Dream of the Sunset? says the voice—suddenly very plain-ly above the sound of the singing Wind. *Young man, this is the Dream of Your Life—THIS is Your Dream of the Sunset. Hear me well, now, for I will be re-turning to visit you often, like this. Hear me well, for this is what I say:*

The Power of the Universe has brought You to where you are. All of Us who are no longer physical—it is Our desire to help our ancestors, who are yet on Earth, to enjoy their physical lives to the fullest. You who have bodies can do wonderful things, there on Earth, that we, who are Spirits, can no longer do ourselves. We can only enjoy those things through the bodies of others—and only those others who know our Spirits and accept them. Those of my ancestors who are there with you now, they already know us. But the People at the places where we brought you from, they are often not aware that anything exists be-yond their bodies. We can not help them to find strength in their lives, because they do not recognize our guidance—though they are our ancestors as well as the People who are right there, with you. For, only the Great Power of the Universe is everlasting—and we are All a part of that Great Power. If those others destroy their bodies—or even this whole Earth—it will be of no consequence to the Great Power of the Universe—for everything will still be a part of that Great Power.

Only the wonderful experience of physical life will be shortened for All who are concerned—their Spirits will join the rest of us in the Universe that much sooner—and they will have that much less happiness to bring with them after they leave their bodies behind.

You, young man, will be going back to your other People, to tell them about the happiness that they can find if they live their lives in harmony with Nature—if they seek to meet and know the many other Spirits who dwell all around them, recognizing the spiritual one-ness of Us All. You will be learning about the Spirits who are guiding others—for All of Us out here in the Universe wish to give guidance to our ancestors back there, on Earth. You will learn about the many other Spirits, and you will tell those who wish to know about Us—the Spirits who will be guiding You.

You must live a simple life—you must live it in accordance to the way we direct you. You will see Us any evening that you sit by yourself, quietly, and watch the ending of the day—for We are the Spirits of the Dream of the Sunset.

The boy who was my son while I lived there, on Earth, is there, now, with You. He has brought back the Sacred Pipe Stem which I once left in the moun-tains for You—for All of You. Long I have known You would be coming—to give Us your body to use. By your words and your actions we can inspire others to join Us in keeping alive our Spirit on the Earth. For We are Your People—we have brought You to Us because we long ago knew that You felt our guidance.

*I, too, was once guided to this life by Spirits more Powerful than I could under-
stand. I once lived far to the South of where we are now. But the Spirits of our
ancestors, even then, felt need of someone on Earth to help keep their Spirit
alive. I, too, had a vision and was given the Dream of the Sunset, which guided
me and brought happiness to my life. I became the Brother of the Sun and travelled far and wide over this land while following the Dream of the Sunset. I
learned much from the different People with whom I camped, ate, hunted, and
prayed. They are all with me now—our Spirits are All together. Often we return
to the places where we dwelled while on Earth—and often we are saddened because no one knows that we are there—no one feels the presence of our Spirits.
Only at Hidden Valley do our ancestors still live in harmony with the Spirits of
Nature—only at Hidden Valley can we give bodies the strength we wish to give
everywhere. Here is how You will help Us:*

*In the Winter to come I will tell you the story of the Dream of the Sunset.
I will tell You about the Powers which I found during my travels here and there.
I will tell you about the People and the places and their legends. You will tell my
story to those back where You came from who care. You will have the Sacred
Pipe Stem as a physical reminder of our Spirits—our Power will be with You that
way. The stories I will tell you are all long ones—of ceremonies, of hunting
parties, of many tribes. You must be patient—hear everything that I tell you—
for when the time comes it will be Your turn to visit there. You will go back to
all those old places—tell others about the Spirits you find there.*

*I cannot yet tell you when you will be returning to your other People—it
may be next Summer, or the one after that. All I can say is that You must first
hear the whole story of my Dream of the Sunset so that You will know where
All those Good Spirits are at. Along with my stories I will show you many of
the People whom I met on my travels—I will show you their ceremonies and
camps. They will sing again the songs they once sang for me—they will tell again
the traditions of their tribes.*

*I will leave You, for now, my Son and Brother, I will leave my Friends
and Sisters behind. I am happy to have brought You to this place, where my
Relatives will All treat you kindly. Look for The Dream of the Sunset—be
patient, for the story takes long to tell. The Power that YOU have found at
Hidden Valley is now ready to help Your Life to be well.*

. . . .With a sudden surge of Power I stand up to dance to the song which
All the Spirits at Hidden Valley are singing—All the Spirits who will make my
Life Strong. In my arms rests the Sacred Pipe Stem—its vibrating plumes make
not a sound—in my head is the Sacred Vibration—making tears from my eyes fall
to the Ground. Each drumbeat flashes through my whole body—causing me to
sway up and down—while the People hold hands in a circle—dancing slowly
around and around. Their faces are beaming with laughter, with smiling, with
glowing happiness—so strong is this Life in Heaven, so Strong is this Life in bliss.

FOR A LISTING OF RELATED BOOKS
WRITE TO:

GOOD MEDICINE BOOKS
BOX 844-C
SKOOKUMCHUCK, B.C.
CANADA
VOB 2E0